C000135095

Mary Berry is well known as the author of more than 35 popular cookery books, including *Mary Berry's New Aga Cookbook*, *The Complete Cookbook*, *Mary Berry Cooks Cakes* and *Cook Now, Eat Later*. She has presented several television cookery series – notably 'Mary Berry at Home' and 'Mary Berry Ultimate Cakes' – and is a regular contributor to BBC2 'Saturday Kitchen' and 'Good Food Live'. She is loved for her practical and unfussy approach to preparing and serving food and is recognised as the queen of Aga cookery. She runs Aga workshops from her home in Buckinghamshire where she also works on her beautiful garden, her other great passion.

'The doyenne of Aga cookery' *Sainsbury's Magazine*

'This is a fantastic cookbook... Her language is so friendly and accessible it's like being shown how to cook by a good friend... A lovely book' *Fresh*

'The queen of no fuss cookery does it again with a collection of foolproof and quick recipes that will save time but still taste utterly delicious' *Homestyle*

Recent books by Mary Berry

The New Cook
Mary Berry Cooks Cakes
Mary Berry at Home
The Complete Cookbook
The Ultimate Cake Book
Quick and Easy Cake Book
Mary Berry's New Aga Cookbook
Cook Now, Eat Later

With my twin granddaughters, Abby, left, and Grace

Mary Berry
real food – *fast*

headline

Copyright © 2005 Mary Berry

Photographs © by Juliet Piddington

The right of Mary Berry to be identified as the Author of the Work has been asserted
by her in accordance with the Copyright, Designs and Patents Act 1988.

First published in 2005
by HEADLINE PUBLISHING GROUP

First published in paperback in 2007
by HEADLINE PUBLISHING GROUP

2

Apart from any use permitted under UK copyright law, this publication may only be
reproduced, stored, or transmitted, in any form, or by any means,with prior permission in
writing of the publishers or, in the case of reprographic production, in accordance with
the terms of licences issued by the Copyright Licensing Agency.

Cataloguing in Publication Data is available from the British Library

ISBN 978 07553 6604 0

Typeset in Avant Garde and Stempel Garamond by Fiona Pike

Printed and bound in the UK by Butler Tanner & Dennis Ltd
Photography by Juliet Piddington

Headline's policy is to use papers that are natural, renewable and recyclable products
and made from wood grown in sustainable forests. The logging and manufacturing
processes are expected to conform to the environmental regulations of the country
of origin.

HEADLINE PUBLISHING Group
An Hachette Livre UK Company
338 Euston Road
London NW1 3BH

www.headline.co.uk
www.hodderheadline.com

Contents

INTRODUCTION

'Real' food is what I have always cooked. Real food consists of fresh meat, poultry, game and fish, of fresh seasonal vegetables and fruit. Real food is cooked simply, without too much complication, with complementary flavourings, to make dishes that I would serve my family and friends for kitchen suppers or lunches, or slightly more formal dinners in the dining room. Real food does not come in packets of ready-assembled, part-cooked ingredients, ready to be heated through in the microwave.

But these days, when so many of us lead such busy lives, those packets are what a lot of harried people turn to, as they feel they have no time to prepare and cook real food, and need to eat something that is fast. The phrase 'fast food' has acquired dubious connotations, but what I think of as 'fast' is something quite different. And you may think that the words 'real' and 'fast' cannot be allied to each other, but in my scheme of things they can. Real food may take longer to prepare and cook than a few minutes in a microwave, but with a little foresight, a bit of planning and some work in advance, real foods can, in essence, be as speedily put on the table as anything else.

Buying good and real ingredients is the first step, and this will always take time, but it's as easy to pick up a couple of steaks or fresh trout as it is to pick up those infamous packets. And while you're at it, you can pick up some of the better ready-prepared foods that are now available to us. Used judiciously, these can add flavour and depth to a basic real food ingredient. I'm thinking about things like jars of roasted peppers or artichokes in oil, tubs of hummus, jars of tapenade or béarnaise sauce, cans of crabmeat or pulses such as cannellini beans, chickpeas or lentils, and cartons of crème fraîche, yoghurt, good

Lucy Young, left, Mary's 'right hand' for over fifteen years

6

vanilla custard (made with cream, of course!), stock or fruit juices. You could also lay your hands on other ready-made ingredients such as frozen puff pastry, ready-to-bake focaccia or ciabatta bread, trifle sponges and pancakes. There is also now a wealth of wonderful oriental products available, such as soy sauce, coconut milk and cream, spices, curry pastes, fish sauce and plum sauce; because of these, my style of cooking has become less classic, and you will find a number of eastern-style influences in the pages to come. (Even my fishcakes have had a lift!) With some of these bought items in your shopping basket – or, more importantly, in your store-cupboard – you can appreciate how real food can become faster food. Ingredients such as these are 'helping hands' to real food, and I for one would never look down my nose at them.

Many of the recipes in the following pages take no time at all to prepare and cook, and some need no cooking at all. But many of the recipes take much longer, and you may think they have no place in a book that promotes itself as being 'fast'. However, that is where the planning comes in: a lasagne, moussaka or other meat stew may take a few hours to cook, but both preparation and cooking can have been done the day before, even two days before, and then all you have to do is reheat the dish when you need it. You cook when you have the time, and then the serving time becomes fast and hassle-free. The same goes for pre-preparation: many foods (vegetables, for instance) can be peeled and cut in advance and stored appropriately; many dishes can be part-prepared or cooked, then stored in the fridge until needed. If you only have to cope with reheating and a few final finishing touches, then I think you will see that real food can indeed become fast food.

Mary Berry

Some Notes about the Recipes

Most of the recipes have some notes after them, which perhaps need some explanation.

GOOD THINGS TO KNOW These notes are a summation of our collective kitchen wisdom – that of Lucy, Lucinda and myself. The three of us tested every single recipe – often more than once, with different ingredients – and anything we thought interesting or informative we have written down. If we used something unusual, we explain what it is; if we thought an ingredient could be used in another way, we mention this. And, by the way, one particularly good thing to know is that all the eggs used throughout the book are large. I do hope you find these notes useful.

PREPARING AHEAD This, in a sense, lies at the heart of the book, and the most important thing to remember is to store the prepared food appropriately. If it has been cooked, it should be allowed to cool, then it must be covered – with foil or clingfilm – and stored in the fridge. When reheating, allow to come to room temperature first or, if time is too short for that, cook straight from the fridge for a slightly longer time. Many foods can be frozen, and again you must remember to allow time for foods to defrost thoroughly before being reheated.

AGA Not all cooked dishes here have Aga notes attached to them, as many of them are cooked in exactly the same way as on an ordinary cooker – by being boiled or simmered on the hob. But when there is a particular Aga technique, we have mentioned it. For instance, something on the Aga can be brought to the boil on the boiling plate, then simmered on the simmering plate. But if that simmering is to continue for more than a few minutes, then the Aga cook would be better putting the dish in the simmering oven. This will take longer than simmering on the top, but – and this is one of the huge advantage of Agas – there is no danger of anything boiling over, and there are no kitchen smells.

Vegetarian Recipes suitable for vegetarians are marked (*V*).

Acknowledgements

I say this every time, but Lucy Young has been with me for 15 years now, and I love her to bits. I cannot imagine life without Lucy: she thinks for me, encourages me, brings the best out in me. She has now become an author herself, and has had enormous success with her first book, *Secrets from a Country Kitchen*. I'm very proud of her.

It's really been a team effort, this book. Lucy is assisted by Lucinda Kaizik. She came to us from Leith's as a keen fledgling four years ago, has an excellent palate, is a very good cook, and what a joy it has been to see her blossom. Lucy and Lucinda have a lot of young friends, and therefore they come with a lot of young ideas, so you will see ingredients in this book that are absolutely of the moment. We make a good team.

Lucy, Lucinda (above) and I have tested all the recipes, have enjoyed them for lunches, and taken them home for supper. Many of the recipes we have developed through the Aga workshops, and some of them I've created for the BBC's *Saturday Kitchen* TV programme. I have really enjoyed working with Antony Worrall Thompson and those dishy chefs, and I think I've learned to cook even more quickly through appearing on the live programme: there is always a competition, for a recipe that can be made in 6 minutes, which viewers vote for. Quite a few of the recipes in this book began in that context.

If developing and cooking recipes are important, so too is the tasting. When we are testing recipes, you can guarantee there is a queue for tasting! Paul, my husband, is an important taster as he is very honest, although he is often happier with bangers and mash! Our young love to taste and give their opinion, and to finish off the leftovers. Tom takes quite a lot home to Sarah and the girls. Annabel and Dan are great entertainers and often cook for friends, so it is lovely to hear of their ideas for cooking for a crowd. My family have always been the most important people to please.

From the publishing point of view, this is the third book I have worked on with the lovely Celia Kent at Headline: Celia keeps us on the straight and narrow, and when the phone rings, we are always delighted, because she is just as enthusiastic about the book as we are. And if the book reads well, it's not due to my English (a subject I didn't pass at school), it's due to Susan Fleming, who has edited most of my books in the last few years and is exceedingly knowledgeable on food and wine. Huge thanks to you both.

I am delighted with the photographs, by Juliet Piddington, wonderfully assisted by the lovely Kim Morphew.

So thank you to everyone above – a wonderful team, and a joy to work with.

CHAPTER 1
SMALL EATS TO GO WITH DRINKS

I love serving little nibbles – or canapés – to go with drinks, but they are usually very time-consuming to make. The answer is a bit of planning in advance. Firstly you must consider how many different eats you are going to prepare. If I were having people in for drinks only, I wouldn't offer too large a choice – perhaps three to five different tastes – and if it is for before an elaborate meal, just one taste only. If you are offering more than one canapé, and you haven't got much time, you needn't feel you have to make them all yourself. There are plenty of things you can buy that will be delicious – good olives in olive oil, for instance, are lovely for people to help themselves. Everyone loves smoked salmon too, and you can serve this in a variety of ways: simply rolling little pieces into tubes takes no time at all. (And don't forget about smoked trout, which is smoked and sliced in the same way as salmon, and is very good.) If you are really short of time you can now buy ready-cooked and peeled quail's eggs too, and I think they make lovely canapés served simply with celery salt or hollandaise sauce.

Some things can be made ready a long time in advance, which will cut down on your working time in the days before your party. Home-made cheese biscuits, for instance (see page 17), can be baked and stored – or frozen – up to a month ahead. It really is a matter of being very well organised. One of the finest tips I can give, though, is to keep the fridge as clear as possible so that you have plenty of space in which to store your home-made eats before serving. And if you entertain often, buy things that keep sensibly. I would always buy wooden cocktail sticks by the hundred, for instance, as they are so very much cheaper. I have jars of really good olives, just in case, including a can or two of olives stuffed with anchovies. And I also keep a few things ready to use for dipping – mini pitta breads or mini garlic breadsticks, which are best kept in the freezer – and, of course, your favourite potato or vegetable crisps as a back-up.

So enjoy preparing your nibbles – they can make a get-together into a party!

Brandade of Hot-Smoked Salmon

Hot-smoked salmon is lightly smoked and has a flaky texture. This brandade mixture can be served on crostini or bruschetta if preferred, or for a starter simply pile on a salad and decorate, or pack into six 7.5cm (3in) cooking rings to give a smart shape.

SERVES 6
Preparation time 10 minutes

3 tablespoons low-fat mayonnaise
3 tablespoons crème fraîche
2 tablespoons tomato ketchup
1 good tablespoon creamed
    horseradish sauce
a good dash of Tabasco sauce
salt and freshly ground black
    pepper
a small bunch of fresh dill,
    chopped
2 hard-boiled eggs, peeled
    and very finely chopped
½ cucumber, peeled, seeded
    and very finely diced
200g (7oz) hot-smoked salmon
    (sometimes called flaky smoked
    salmon)
2 tablespoons chopped fresh
    parsley

TO SERVE
1 packet sliced pumpernickel
    rye bread
3 teaspoons black lumpfish caviar
lots of fresh dill sprigs

PREPARING AHEAD *These can be prepared and finished the day before. Keep the pieces very close together on a platter to prevent drying out. Cover with clingfilm and store in the fridge.*

1 Measure the mayonnaise, crème fraîche, ketchup, horseradish, Tabasco, seasoning and dill into a mixing bowl. Gently fold in the chopped egg, cucumber, large flakes of salmon and parsley.

2 Cut each slice of the rye bread into six even-sized pieces. Top each with a teaspoon of the brandade.

3 Spoon a little caviar on, and top with a sprig of dill.

GOOD THINGS TO KNOW *Sometimes hot-smoked salmon is sold in the piece and sometimes ready flaked. If in the piece it keeps better and all that has to be done is to remove the skin, which peels off very easily. Any mixture left over can be used in sandwich fillings.*

Quail's Egg and Hollandaise Mini Tartlets

It is very time-consuming making tiny pastry cases, but you can buy some very good ones in supermarkets and delicatessens. Avoid wafer cases (like ice-cream wafers), as these are not so nice.

MAKES 24
Preparation time 10 minutes
Cooking time 12 minutes

24 mini cocktail pastry cases

FILLING

12 quail's eggs
24 small asparagus tips
salt and freshly ground black
  pepper
a little bought olive tapenade
a little bought good hollandaise
  sauce
paprika
a little melted butter

Preheat the oven to 150°C/
Fan 130°C/Gas 2.

PREPARING AHEAD *They can be prepared about 6 hours ahead, but not longer than that, or they can go soggy.*

1 Boil the eggs in boiling water for about 2 minutes (this will give a soft yolk), drain and refresh in cold water. Peel at once, carefully, as they are soft-boiled.

2 Blanch the asparagus tips in boiling salted water until just tender. Refresh in cold water, and dry using kitchen paper.

3 Spoon a little olive tapenade into the base of each pastry case.

4 Carefully slice each quail's egg in half lengthways and put one-half in the base of each case, yolk side up. Season, spoon over a little hollandaise sauce, and sprinkle with paprika. Top with the asparagus tips and brush with a little melted butter.

5 Arrange on a small baking sheet and heat through in the preheated oven for about 12 minutes until warm. Serve warm.

GOOD THINGS TO KNOW *If preferred, you can replace the olive tapenade with sun-dried tomato paste or pesto. Quail's eggs are difficult to peel if very fresh, so buy them a week ahead and keep them in the fridge.*

AGA Heat in the simmering oven for about 10 minutes.

Prawn Bloody Marys on Chinese Spoons

These are so unusual, but very quick to do. The recipe makes enough for about 40 bites, but they will keep well in the fridge. Chinese spoons are impressive and very up-to-the-minute for drinks parties. If you haven't got any china spoons, serve in scooped-out cherry tomatoes or celery boats.

MAKES ABOUT 40

Preparation time 10 minutes, plus setting time

40 shelled cooked prawns
a few snipped fresh chives

SAUCE
3 tablespoons vodka
a dash of Tabasco sauce
1 tablespoon Worcestershire sauce
1 tablespoon creamed horseradish
   sauce
425ml (15fl oz) tomato juice
celery salt and freshly ground
   black pepper
2 tablespoons water
1 x 11g packet powdered gelatine

1 Measure the vodka into a measuring jug, then add the Tabasco, Worcestershire and horseradish sauces. Make up to 500ml (18fl oz) with tomato juice. Season with celery salt and pepper.

2 Measure the water into a small ramekin and sprinkle over the gelatine. Stir and set aside to 'sponge'.

3 Bring the tomato juice mixture up to the boil in a saucepan. Add the sponged gelatine to the hot liquid and whisk until smooth. Pour into a heatproof bowl, cool, then leave to set in the fridge.

4 Using an ordinary teaspoon, spoon out a little of the set jelly and sit on a china spoon. Arrange a prawn and some chives on top, and serve cold.

GOOD THINGS TO KNOW *The bites will stay firm on the spoons for up to 8 hours, but do keep them in the fridge. If you only have half the amount of spoons, wash them up and refill, or do half in spoons and half in halved and scooped-out tomatoes.*

Prawn Bloody Marys, left, Quail's Egg and Hollandaise Mini Tartlets, far right, and Tortilla Tapas

Tortilla Tapas (V)

Bought tortillas are usually about 18cm (7in) in diameter; if yours are smaller, you may need two. This topping mixture can also be put on blinis, which are available in supermarkets.

MAKES 24 CANAPES
Preparation time 10 minutes
Cooking time 5 minutes

1 tortilla wrap

TOPPING

1 x 100g tub hummus
75g (3oz) feta cheese, crumbled
12 black olives in oil, halved and stoned
6 sun-blushed tomatoes, snipped into quarters with scissors
24 small fresh parsley sprigs

PREPARING AHEAD *These little canapés can be prepared up to 8 hours ahead so long as the tortilla is crisp before you put the filling on top.*

1 Toast the tortilla in a hot, dry, non-stick frying pan over high heat until golden brown and crisp on each side. Set aside to cool.

2 Using a 3cm (1 ¼in) scone cutter, cut 24 circles from the tortilla.

3 Spread the discs with a thin layer of hummus. Top with a little feta, half an olive, a piece of sun-blushed tomato and a sprig of parsley.

4 To serve, reheat in a very low oven or gently under the grill for about 5 minutes just to warm through.

GOOD THINGS TO KNOW *You can use either sun-dried or sun-blushed tomatoes for this recipe. They are very similar, but the sun-blushed are a little softer.*

AGA Reheat in the simmering oven for about 5-8 minutes until warm.

City Slickers

These are very quick canapés to make well ahead, ready to serve cold. You can pick up all the ingredients in the supermarket very easily; they take no time to put together, and they also look very pretty. You will need 20 cocktail sticks.

MAKES 20
Preparation time 10 minutes

20 thin round slices salami
2 tablespoons cream cheese
freshly ground black pepper
20 small gherkins, each cut into 5

PREPARING AHEAD *You can make them a day ahead, and keep them, covered with clingfilm, in the fridge.*

1 Take each disc of salami and spread with a thin layer of cream cheese. Sprinkle with black pepper.

2 Put a gherkin in the centre of each disc of salami and roll into a cigar shape. Hold in place with a cocktail stick.

GOOD THINGS TO KNOW *You can use a variety of different meats – pastrami, chorizo, Parma or other dry-cured ham – to your taste. Whichever you use, it needs to be thinly sliced. You could also vary the flavours of the cream cheese. The meats could be wrapped around pitted olives instead of the gherkins, if preferred.*

Parmesan and Pistachio Nutters (v)

A wonderful biscuit, for nibbles with a glass of wine before dinner. Do be careful not to overcook them, as they burn very easily!

MAKES ABOUT 40
Preparation time 10 minutes
Cooking time 15-20 minutes

100g (4 oz) butter, very soft
50g (2 oz) semolina
85g (3 ½ oz) self-raising flour
75g (3 oz) Parmesan, grated
a good pinch of dry mustard
   powder
salt and freshly ground black
   pepper
40 small pistachio nuts

Preheat the oven to 180ºC/
Fan 160ºC/Gas 4.

PREPARING AHEAD *These freeze brilliantly, just defrost and refresh in a medium oven to crisp them up before serving. They can also be made up to a week ahead and kept in an airtight container lined with kitchen paper.*

1 Measure all the ingredients, except the nuts, into a large bowl and work together until combined to a soft dough. This can also be done in a food processor.

2 Roll the dough into about 40 small balls. Arrange on a large baking sheet and press so they resemble a very thick £1 coin. Press a nut into the centre of each.

3 Bake in the preheated oven for about 15-20 minutes until pale golden brown – you will need to keep an eye on them! Cool on a wire rack and serve cold.

GOOD THINGS TO KNOW *You can use other nuts to top the biscuits. I have an aversion to peanuts, but you could use them, or why not try cashews or pine nuts instead of the pistachios?*

AND ANOTHER THING *You can also use 2 teaspoons to spoon out blobs – these will not be perfectly shaped but at least they look home-made!*

AGA Bake on the grid shelf on the floor of the roasting oven, with the cold sheet on the second set of runners for about 12-15 minutes until pale golden brown.

Smoked Salmon and Cream Cheese Bites

The biscuits can be bought in any good supermarket in the crisps, nuts and savoury biscuit section. Some supermarkets now sell these toasts under their own name, but they seem just the same to me.

MAKES 20
Preparation time 10 minutes

20 Mini Morceaux garlic toasts
50g (2oz) full-fat cream cheese
finely grated rind of ½ lemon
freshly ground black pepper
2 slices smoked salmon
20 small sprigs fresh dill

PREPARING AHEAD *These are wonderful as they can be made well ahead, and stay lovely and crisp – but only if you use full-fat cream cheese. If you were making them to serve straightaway, you could use half fat.*

1 Take each toast and spread a little cream cheese on the top.

2 Sprinkle with a little grated lemon rind and black pepper.

3 Snip the smoked salmon into thin strips, using scissors and arrange a piece on the top.

4 Garnish with a sprig of dill and serve cold.

GOOD THINGS TO KNOW *For a change, spread the toasts with green pesto, tapenade or sun-dried tomato paste and top with mozzarella or Parma ham. Use the best smoked salmon you can for this recipe, not the trimmings.*

Mini Sausages with Mango Chutney and Sesame

These are our favourite eats to do at any time of year. They are popular with all age groups, and if you want to be particularly clever, put wooden cocktail sticks in them, and stick them into a cottage loaf. You can reheat them and the loaf in the oven at the same time.

MAKES 10
Preparation time 5 minutes
Cooking time 20 minutes

20 cocktail sausages
2 tablespoons mango chutney
25g (1oz) sesame seeds

Preheat the oven to 200°C/ Fan 180°C/Gas 6, or preheat the grill – whichever you prefer. Lightly grease a roasting tin or line the grill pan with foil.

PREPARING AHEAD *These can be made up to a day ahead, reheated and sprinkled with sesame seeds to serve.*

1 Arrange the sausages in a roasting tin, in one layer.

2 Roast in the preheated oven for about 15-20 minutes until golden brown and cooked through. Turn over halfway through.

3 Remove from the oven and tip into a bowl, making sure no excess fat from the pan is added. Stir in the mango chutney to coat the sausages.

4 Sprinkle over the sesame seeds, and serve the sausages warm with cocktail sticks.

GOOD THINGS TO KNOW *Be sure to add the mango chutney while the sausages are hot so it sticks to them.*

AGA Slide the greased roasting tin on to the floor of the roasting oven and cook for about 15 minutes until golden brown and cooked through. Turn over halfway through.

Dips in Minutes (V)

Red Pepper and Herb Process 2 canned red peppers, drained, with 2 roughly chopped spring onions, a small bunch of fresh basil, and a few sprigs each of parsley and dill in a processor for a few minutes. Add 8 tablespoons low-calorie mayonnaise and process again, then season with salt and pepper to taste. Put into a serving bowl, cover with clingfilm and chill. Can be made up to three days ahead and kept in the fridge.

Spiced Mango Process 225g (8oz) half-fat cream cheese with 1 tablespoon curry powder, 4 tablespoons mango chutney and the juice of ½ lemon, and season with salt and pepper to taste. Put into a serving bowl, cover with clingfilm and chill. Can be made up to three days ahead and kept in the fridge.

Guacamole Peel a large ripe avocado, and cut the flesh into chunks. Coarsely chop 4 spring onions. Peel and deseed 2 large firm tomatoes, put them into the processor with the other ingredients and whiz until smooth. Add a dash each of Tabasco, sugar and lemon juice, plus some salt and pepper to taste, and whiz again. Put into a serving bowl, cover with clingfilm and chill. Make on the day of serving.

Blue Cheese Measure 100g (4oz) Dolcelatte or Stilton cheese into the processor, add a 150ml carton soured cream and a little pepper and whiz – just as simple as that!

Put into a serving bowl, cover with clingfilm and chill. Can be made up to three days ahead and kept in the fridge.

Mild Chilli Mix a 200ml carton of low-fat crème fraîche with 4 tablespoons bought chilli dipping sauce, stir well, and season with salt and pepper. Perfect with prawns or chicken goujons. Put into a serving bowl, cover with clingfilm and chill. Can be made up to three days ahead and kept in the fridge.

GOOD THINGS FOR DIPPING

Vegetables Pencil thickness and about 7.5cm (3in) long sticks of carrot, red or yellow pepper, courgette, cucumber or celery. Halved baby sweetcorn and tiny mangetout or sugar-snap peas are ideal too.

Garlic Pitta Bread Melt 50g (2oz) butter and mix with 2 crushed garlic cloves. Brush this over the cut side of 4 large pitta breads, split in half horizontally. Arrange on a foil-lined grill pan and sprinkle with salt and pepper. Slide under the grill and cook for about 5 minutes until golden brown and crispy. Slice into triangles and serve.

To cook in the AGA, arrange on a baking sheet and slide on to the top set of runners for about 6 minutes until golden brown.

Bread sticks These are ideal for dipping – but a little boring!

Dips, left to right: Red Pepper and Herb, Blue Cheese, Spiced Mango, Mild Chilli, and Guacamole

Pesto and Cheese Focaccia Eats (V)

These can be served hot or cold, but I prefer them hot. You could serve a pile of them with a dip or a variety of dips (see page 21).

MAKES 20
Preparation time 10 minutes
Cooking time 10 minutes

1 ready-to-bake focaccia bread
50g (2oz) butter, softened
2 garlic cloves, crushed
50g (2oz) Parmesan, grated
2 tablespoons green pesto
2 tablespoons chopped fresh
    parsley

Preheat the oven to 200°C/
Fan 180°C/Gas 6.

PREPARING AHEAD *This can be made the day before and reheated to serve.*

1 Put the focaccia on a baking sheet.

2 Mix all the remaining ingredients together and spread over the focaccia.

3 Bake in the preheated oven for about 10-12 minutes until golden brown.

4 Slice the focaccia into 20 small squares and serve warm.

GOOD THINGS TO KNOW *We are so lucky with the different breads we can buy. For a change you could try this recipe with some of the flavoured breads, e.g. olive bread or sun-dried tomato bread.*

AGA Slide the baking sheet on to the second set of runners in the roasting oven for about 10 minutes.

CHAPTER 2
FIRST COURSES

Most of the dishes in this chapter, apart from the soups, can be made in about 10-15 minutes, and many of them can be prepared quite a bit in advance, so long as they are covered in clingfilm and stored in the fridge. Many assembled first courses are actually better served slightly chilled anyway. And of course, any dressings usually benefit from being made well in advance, then poured over salads just before serving, otherwise the leaves will wilt.

I always think something like a salad first course is better served on individual plates, and these can be done ahead, covered with clingfilm. But if you haven't room in the fridge, most of the recipes can be adapted to be served on a large platter (an idea which crops up quite a bit here). This is especially useful if you are catering for a smaller number: different foods can be arranged in groups, and people can just help themselves. Last year we had a New Year's Eve party here at home. There were twelve of us, and everyone did their bit, bringing their own specialities, resulting in a wonderful meal. I shall long remember Jenny walking in with a spectacular, huge flat oval dish with an assembly of groups of smoked salmon, smoked eel, trout, prawns, a little rocket and asparagus too, with, in the middle, a bowl of herb mayonnaise. So simple and very, very special, and she even remembered the lemons and brown bread and butter – all great fun.

Soups can mostly be made ahead, and indeed frozen, and many of the things you might offer to accompany a soup or first course – such as garlic bread – can also be made ahead and frozen.

Butternut Squash Soup (V)

Unlike pumpkins, butternut squashes are available all year. Shaped like a large peanut, they have a sweet orange flesh. Roasting them first in the oven means that you don't have to tackle removing the tough skin, and it fills the kitchen with a delicious aroma! The soup freezes well too. If you are a gardener, butternut squashes are easier to grow than courgettes, but they take up a lot of room and love lots of water and sunshine. In fact, you could find yourself with far too many!

SERVES 6

Preparation time 15 minutes
Cooking time 1 hour 20 minutes

3 small butternut squashes, about
   1.6kg (3 ½lb) total weight
about 2 tablespoons olive oil
salt and freshly ground black
   pepper
freshly grated nutmeg
25g (1oz) butter
1 large onion, roughly chopped
2 large carrots, roughly chopped
2 large celery sticks, sliced
2.5cm (1in) piece fresh root ginger,
   grated
1.2-1.3 litres (2-2 ¼ pints) vegetable
   stock
leaves from 1 sprig fresh rosemary,
   chopped, or 1 teaspoon dried
   rosemary

Preheat the oven to 200°C/
Fan 180°C/Gas 6.

PREPARING AHEAD *Make a lot of this in advance – especially if you have squashes growing in the garden – and freeze in suitable quantities.*

1 Cut the butternut squashes in half lengthways, scoop out the seeds with a metal spoon and discard. Arrange the squash halves cut-side up in a roasting tin just big enough to hold them in a single layer, and drizzle over the olive oil. Season each squash half with salt, pepper and freshly grated nutmeg. Pour 150ml (¼ pint) water around the squash. Roast in the preheated oven for about an hour or until tender. Allow to cool.

2 Melt the butter in a large pan and add the onion, carrot, celery and grated ginger. Cook over a high heat for a few minutes, stirring continuously. Add the stock, rosemary and seasoning, and bring to the boil for a few minutes. Cover and simmer for about 20 minutes until the vegetables are tender.

3 When cool enough to handle, scoop the flesh from the squash skins and add to the pan. Blend the vegetables in a liquidiser or food processor until smooth.

4 Taste for seasoning and serve hot with crusty bread.

GOOD THINGS TO KNOW *This recipe can also be made with pumpkin when in season. Just cut into large chunks and roast in the preheated oven as above.*

AND ANOTHER THING *If you are not a fan of totally puréed soup, when the onion, carrot and celery are tender, lift some out with a slotted spoon and do not purée with the rest. Keep to one side then return to the main puréed soup before serving.*

AGA Slide the squash halves in a roasting tin on to the second runners of the roasting oven for about an hour, basting occasionally, until very tender. To cook the vegetables, bring to the boil on the boiling plate, cover and transfer to the simmering oven for about 20 minutes.

Pea, Horseradish and Coriander Soup (V)

This sounds a strange combination of ingredients, but it works well, and this will be one of the fastest soups you have ever made.

SERVES 6
Preparation time 5 minutes
Cooking time 15 minutes

1 tablespoon olive oil
1 large onion, finely chopped
900ml (1 ½ pints) vegetable stock
450g (1lb) frozen peas
2 level tablespoons creamed
   horseradish sauce
a good pinch of caster sugar
a good dash of Tabasco sauce
2 tablespoons chopped fresh
   coriander
3 tablespoons cream, single or
   double

PREPARING AHEAD *If not serving at once, cool and keep in the fridge – without the cream – then reheat quickly, stirring, and serve straightaway. The soup can also be frozen, again without the final toppings.*

1 Heat the oil in a pan, add the onion, and cook for a few minutes. Cover and simmer until the onion is soft and transparent, about 10 minutes, stirring from time to time.

2 Add the stock and bring to the boil. Add the peas to the boiling stock and onion and simmer for about 3 minutes until the peas are tender.

3 Allow to cool slightly, then ladle into a processor and whiz until the soup is very smooth. Add the horseradish, sugar and Tabasco, and dilute with a little more stock if too thick.

4 Just before serving add the chopped coriander and swirl the cream on top.

GOOD THINGS TO KNOW *Pea, spinach and watercress soups lose a little of their vibrant colour if kept hot for a long time.*

Chunky Vegetable and Spaghetti Soup (V)

This is a quick, heart-warming soup. It's full of flavour but as there is no fat, it is healthy too!

SERVES 6
Preparation time 10 minutes
Cooking time 15 minutes

3 large shallots, sliced
2 large carrots, peeled and
   chopped into 2.5cm (1in) dice
2 large parsnips, peeled and
   chopped into 2.5cm (1in) dice
3 celery sticks, thinly sliced
2 fat garlic cloves, crushed
2 x 400g cans chopped tomatoes
1.7 litres (3 pints) vegetable stock
50g (2oz) spaghetti, broken into
   about 4cm (1 ¾in) pieces
2 tablespoons sun-dried tomato
   paste
2 teaspoons caster sugar
50g (2oz) fresh white breadcrumbs
salt and freshly ground black
   pepper
a bunch of fresh basil leaves,
   roughly chopped
freshly grated Parmesan (optional)

PREPARING AHEAD *This soup is best not frozen, but you can prepare a couple of days in advance, without the basil and Parmesan.*

1 Put the prepared vegetables, garlic, tomatoes and stock into a large deep saucepan.

2 Bring the soup up to the boil, add the spaghetti and continue to boil for about 10 minutes until the vegetables are tender and the pasta is soft.

3 Add the sun-dried tomato paste, sugar and breadcrumbs to the saucepan and season well with salt and pepper.

4 Serve the hot soup in individual bowls, and sprinkle over the fresh basil leaves and a little grated Parmesan if liked. Serve with warm crusty bread.

GOOD THINGS TO KNOW *Adding fresh white breadcrumbs to soups helps to thicken them when you are not using flour (as in flour-based soups). Make a whole batch of breadcrumbs, keep sealed in a bag in the freezer, and help yourself when you need some.*

Ten-minute Beetroot Soup

So quick to make, and delicious served hot or cold – I slightly prefer it hot. Beetroot is more popular than you may imagine.

SERVES 4-6
Preparation time 5 minutes
Cooking time 10 minutes

1 tablespoon sunflower oil
1 large onion, finely chopped
2 x 250g packets cooked and
   peeled beetroot, roughly
   chopped
1.2 litres (2 pints) chicken stock
150ml (¼ pint) soured cream
1 tablespoon creamed horseradish
   sauce
1 tablespoon balsamic vinegar
salt and freshly ground black
   pepper
2 tablespoons snipped fresh chives

PREPARING AHEAD *Make a day ahead and store in the fridge. It's best not frozen.*

1 Heat the oil in a large deep saucepan, add the onion and fry over a high heat for a few minutes. Lower the heat, cover and simmer for about 5 minutes until the onion is soft.

2 Add the beetroot to the onion. Pour in the stock, bring to the boil, and simmer for a couple of minutes. Cool slightly.

3 Carefully pour into a processor and purée until smooth. Add the soured cream, horseradish, balsamic vinegar, salt and pepper. Whiz once more.

4 Just before serving add the chives and serve with a swirl of extra horseradish if liked.

GOOD THINGS TO KNOW *If you have beetroot in the garden, of course use any surplus for soup. To cook beetroot, leave on 4cm (1 ½in) of leaves on the top and the root, cover and simmer in a pan slowly until tender, from 30 minutes to 3 hours, depending on the size of the beetroot. Do not trim before cooking as the beetroot bleeds and loses its vibrant colour.*

Tomato and Lentil Soup (V)

This is the quickest of soups to make. Lentils in cans are perfect for this recipe, much easier than dried lentils which need to be soaked before using. Be sure to drain and rinse the lentils well.

SERVES 4-6
Preparation time 5 minutes
Cooking time 12 minutes

1 tablespoon sunflower oil
1 large onion, finely chopped
2 garlic cloves, crushed
2 x 400g cans chopped tomatoes
1.2 litres (2 pints) vegetable stock
1 x 410g can lentils, drained and rinsed
1 teaspoon chopped fresh thyme
2 teaspoons caster sugar
2 tablespoons tomato purée
salt and freshly ground black pepper
chopped fresh parsley or basil, for garnish

PREPARING AHEAD *The soup freezes well, and can be kept in the fridge for a couple of days.*

1 Heat the oil in a large saucepan. Add the onion and garlic and fry for 2-3 minutes. Add the tomatoes, stock, lentils, thyme, sugar, tomato purée and seasoning, and bring to the boil.

2 Cover and gently boil for about 10 minutes or until the onions are soft.

3 Carefully ladle the soup into a processor and whiz until smooth (this may need to be done in two batches).

4 Check the seasoning and sprinkle over the parsley or basil just before serving.

GOOD THINGS TO KNOW *Italian canned tomatoes are the best to use in recipes, except when there is a glut of fresh tomatoes at the end of the summer. Fresh ones will need skinning, though, unless the recipe is sieved. I prefer to buy canned tomatoes without added garlic or herbs, as I like to add my own flavourings as I cook.*

Celeriac, Leek and Sweet Potato Soup (V)

A wonderful warming soup using winter vegetables, which is full of flavour.
Cut the vegetables up the same size so they cook at the same rate and will be tender
at the same time. You could use ordinary potatoes instead of the sweet potatoes.

SERVES 4-6

Preparation time 10 minutes
Cooking time 20 minutes

25g (1oz) butter
2 leeks, sliced
750g (1 ¾ lb) celeriac, peeled and
    cut into 1cm (½in) cubes
350g (12oz) sweet potatoes,
    peeled and cut into 1cm (½in)
    cubes
25g (1oz) plain flour
2 litres (3 ½ pints) chicken or
    vegetable stock
salt and freshly ground black
    pepper
3 tablespoons pouring cream

PREPARING AHEAD *The soup*
freezes very well without the
cream. You could also keep it in
the fridge for a couple of days.

1 Melt the butter in a deep saucepan. Add the vegetables, and fry over a medium heat for a few moments without colouring. Add the flour and stir over a high heat for about 2 minutes.

2 Blend in the stock, cover with a lid, bring to the boil and boil for about 10-15 minutes or until the vegetables are tender. Season with salt and pepper.

3 Ladle the soup into a processor and whiz until smooth (you may need to do this in batches).

4 Return to the pan, stir in the cream, and heat through. Check the seasoning and serve.

GOOD THINGS TO KNOW *When puréeing soup in*
a processor, save yourself time by only processing the
vegetables and not the liquid. Strain the liquid off and
add back with the soup when reheating. A blender/
liquidiser will purée better if you use more liquid with
the vegetables.

Smoked Duck Salad with Oriental Sauce

Smoked duck is found sliced in vacuum packs on the deli counter in good supermarkets. It's well worth trying, and it's very good for open sandwiches too.

SERVES 4

Preparation time 10 minutes

½ cucumber, peeled, seeded and sliced into thin 5cm (2in) long strips

4 spring onions, sliced into thin 5cm (2in) long strips

1 x 50g packet lamb's lettuce

1x 100g packet smoked duck breast, trimmed of any fat, thinly sliced

FOR THE DRESSING

1 teaspoon grainy mustard

2 teaspoons honey

2 teaspoons soy sauce

2 teaspoons white wine vinegar

1 tablespoon olive oil

salt and freshly ground black pepper

PREPARING AHEAD *Chill the salad in a bowl (undressed), covered with clingfilm. Slice the duck breasts, wrap tightly in clingfilm, chill and make the dressing. Just before serving dress and toss salad and arrange on plates.*

1 Mix the cucumber, spring onions and lamb's lettuce together in a bowl.

2 Measure the dressing ingredients together, season with salt and pepper, and whisk to combine. Pour over the bowl of salad and toss well.

3 Arrange the salad in the centre of four plates. Carefully arrange the duck slices on top of the lettuce in an attractive way.

GOOD THINGS TO KNOW *Use a potato peeler to remove the skin of a cucumber. Then cut the cucumber in half lengthways, and scoop out the seeds by using your thumb or a teaspoon. This will give attractive horseshoe shapes when sliced across the width of the cucumber.*

Antipasto of Continental Meats

Choose meats that you enjoy most. If serving as a main course, add some cheeses too if you like, and perhaps some fresh figs by the Parma ham.

SERVES 6
Preparation time 10 minutes

175g (6oz) mixed olives
1 x 175g jar artichokes in oil
4 tablespoons balsamic vinegar
4 tablespoons olive oil
6 slices pastrami
12 slices salami
6 slices Parma ham
12 thin slices chorizo
1 x 50g bag rocket

PREPARING AHEAD *The meats can be arranged up to 12 hours ahead on a large platter that will fit into the fridge. Cover with clingfilm.*

1 Put the olives and artichokes into two small bowls or ramekins.

2 Measure the vinegar and oil into a third ramekin, then place all the ramekins near the centre on a large round plate, in a triangle shape.

3 Arrange the meats separately between the gaps, curling the Parma ham and pastrami so they are loosely draped on the plate.

4 Place the rocket in the middle of the plate, and serve with warm Italian bread.

GOOD THINGS TO KNOW *Look out for vacuum packs of mixed sliced continental meats. They are useful if you are making smaller platters: you want them to be varied without having to have every different meat sliced and weighed out separately at the deli counter.*

Mild Chilli Tiger Prawn and Avocado Salad

A modern variation on the classic prawn cocktail, but with a hint of Thai, made more piquant by the addition of fresh red chilli. If you wanted it really hot, you could add a bit of Tabasco as well.

SERVES 4

Preparation time 10 minutes

½ large avocado pear, peeled and cut into small cubes
1 mild red chilli
225g (8oz) cooked tiger prawns, peeled
2 little gem lettuces
fresh parsley leaves (optional)

FOR THE DRESSING
2 tablespoons low-calorie mayonnaise
2 tablespoons crème fraîche
2 tablespoons creamed horseradish sauce
2 tablespoons tomato ketchup

PREPARING AHEAD *This is so easy to assemble, it's best done at the last minute. But the dressing and avocado could be done a couple of hours in advance.*

1 To make the dressing, mix all the ingredients together. Toss the avocado in the dressing and set aside.

2 Slice the chilli in half lengthways, and remove the seeds. Finely chop half the chilli and stir into the dressing. Finely slice the remaining chilli and reserve for garnish.

3 Mix half the prawns in with the avocado and dressing.

4 Arrange 3 lettuce leaves in the centre of each plate in a star shape. Spoon a quarter of the dressing mixture into the middle of the leaves, and top with a quarter of the remaining prawns. Sprinkle over the chilli strips and garnish with parsley, if liked.

GOOD THINGS TO KNOW *Large raw and translucent tiger prawns come from warm climes, and are black when they are raw, pink when cooked. Buy as fresh as possible – ideally uncooked – and cook them yourself.*

Marinated Salmon with Chilli and Lime

This raw marinated fish is not unlike sushi, which is loved by many. It is essential, however, to use really fresh salmon.

SERVES 4-6

Preparation time 10 minutes, plus marinating time

½ red chilli, seeded and finely
   chopped
juice of 1 lime
1 tablespoon soy sauce
2 tablespoons snipped fresh dill
1 teaspoon caster sugar
350g (12oz) salmon fillet, skinned
salt and freshly ground black
   pepper
a few small lettuce leaves
a few sprigs of fresh dill

PREPARING AHEAD *You can prepare individual plates up to 3 hours ahead.*

1 Mix together in a bowl the chilli, lime juice, soy sauce, dill and sugar.

2 Thinly slice the salmon lengthways into very thin strips.

3 Toss the salmon in the marinade and season well. Leave to marinate in the fridge for about 3 hours. Check the seasoning.

4 Serve as a first course on lettuce leaves. Arrange the leaves in individual shallow bowls or on plates. Pile the salmon in the centre and top with a sprig of fresh dill.

GOOD THINGS TO KNOW *Fresh dill is one of my favourite herbs. It's easy to grow in the summer, but rapidly goes to seed, so keep picking, and sow again at six-week intervals from early May until late July. Once picked, keep in a jug of water in the fridge covered with a poly bag.*

Warm Trout Hollandaise Croustades

This is a very smart first course, quick to do and very impressive. Every stage of the recipe can be made ahead and assembled just before warming in the oven. If preferred, serve on a disc of cooked puff pastry.

SERVES 6
Preparation time 10 minutes
Cooking time 15 minutes to serve
warm

6 slices medium-sliced white bread
25g (1oz) butter, melted
2 x 5oz (150g) smoked trout fillets,
   skinned
2 tablespoons chopped fresh dill
1 x 170g jar hollandaise sauce
salt and freshly ground black
   pepper
12 quail's eggs
a little black lumpfish caviar
fresh dill sprigs to garnish

Preheat the oven to 140°C/Fan
120°C/Gas 1.

PREPARING AHEAD The bread croustades can be made ahead. You can top them at the last minute, and heat through in the low oven while you are having drinks.

1 Cut out 6 circles of bread (avoiding the crusts), using a 10cm (4in) round cutter. Brush both sides of the bread with melted butter and place on a baking sheet.

2 Slide under a medium grill for about 3 minutes on each side or until golden brown and crisp, or fry gently until brown in a frying pan (turning the bread halfway through).

3 Flake the smoked trout into a bowl (remove any small bones if necessary) and mix with the dill and 3 tablespoons of the hollandaise sauce. Season with a little salt and black pepper.

4 Cook the quail's eggs in boiling water for 1 ½ minutes to soft-boiled, then drain and submerge in cold water to stop the cooking. Peel straightaway (the shell comes off easier if it is done at once).

5 Divide the trout mixture between the 6 circles of crispy bread, top with 2 peeled eggs and spoon over 1 tablespoon hollandaise so the eggs are covered.

6 To heat through, slide into the low preheated oven for about 15 minutes until warm.

7 Arrange on individual plates, and top with a little caviar and a sprig of dill.

GOOD THINGS TO KNOW You can find smoked trout fillets vacuum-packed in good supermarkets. They usually have the skin on, so remove before flaking. Do not add too much salt as the fish and hollandaise can be quite salty.

AGA Heat in the simmering oven for about 15 minutes until warm.

Smoked Trout and Horseradish Terrine

A pretty first course, that can be made well ahead. Smoked trout slices come in packs similar to smoked salmon. Use smoked salmon if you prefer, but I think trout makes a nice change.

SERVES ABOUT 8

Preparation time 15 minutes, plus chilling time

250g (9oz) smoked trout slices
freshly ground black pepper
225g (8oz) full-fat cream cheese
100g (4oz) unsalted butter, softened
2 tablespoons creamed horseradish sauce
4 anchovy fillets
1-2 tablespoons chopped fresh parsley

PREPARING AHEAD

You can make smoked fish pâtés and terrines up to two days ahead, and keep them in the coldest part of the fridge.

1. Dampen a small 450g (1lb) loaf tin and line generously with clingfilm. Divide the sliced trout into four equal piles. Using one pile, cover the base of the tin with a layer of smoked trout slices, and sprinkle with black pepper.

2. Measure the cheese, butter, horseradish, anchovy fillets and parsley into a processor and whiz until very smooth. Add some pepper (there's no need for salt).

3. Spread a third of the paste over the base layer of fish, and cover with a second layer of smoked trout. Continue with alternative layers, finishing with a layer of smoked trout (four layers smoked trout, three layers cheese paste). Tightly pull the clingfilm over the top and press down firmly. Transfer to the fridge for at least 6 hours, preferably overnight.

4. Turn out, keep in the clingfilm and freeze for about 30 minutes to make slicing easier. Don't be tempted to freeze for longer as the filling would be grainy and wet on thawing.

5. Serve in slices on dressed salad leaves with lemon wedges and buttered brown bread.

GOOD THINGS TO KNOW *If you haven't got any creamed horseradish sauce (from a jar), and only have a stronger variety, just use a little less plus a little double cream. You have to slice the terrine very carefully, as it contains no gelatine and can be very soft. A serrated knife will help.*

Pan-fried Fish Croquettes

These are a sort of mini fishcake with a difference – made with breadcrumbs instead of mashed potato (which gives them a firmer texture) – and they are full of flavour.

MAKES ABOUT 18 TINY CROQUETTES
Preparation time 10 minutes
Cooking time about 6 minutes

3 slices white bread, crusts removed
225g (8oz) cod fillet, skinned and chopped into large pieces
75g (3oz) mature Cheddar, grated
1 tablespoon grainy mustard
a dash of Tabasco sauce
freshly ground black pepper
1 egg, beaten
2 spring onions, finely sliced
1 tablespoon chopped fresh parsley
2 tablespoons sunflower oil

PREPARING AHEAD *Make the raw croquettes a day ahead, store in the fridge, and fry when needed.*

1 Break the bread into a processor and whiz for a few seconds to make fine breadcrumbs. Remove 50g (2oz) breadcrumbs for later.

2 Add the cod, cheese, mustard, Tabasco and black pepper to the processor and whiz again, adding a little beaten egg, until all the ingredients combine and are smooth.

3 Tip the mixture into a bowl, stir in the spring onions and parsley and mix together (I find this easiest to do with my hands). Shape into 18 small croquettes using a dessertspoon, and coat in the remaining breadcrumbs.

4 Heat a little oil in a large frying pan and cook the cakes for about 3-4 minutes, turning, until golden brown all over and cooked through.

5 Serve hot with salad and tarragon mayonnaise (see below).

GOOD THINGS TO KNOW *To make a tarragon mayonnaise, mix 6 tablespoons good mayonnaise with a teaspoon of tarragon vinegar, a few chopped capers, a dash of caster sugar and 2 tablespoons chopped fresh tarragon.*

Mediterranean Crab Tians

Crab lovers will thoroughly approve of this first course. If you prefer prawns, the tians can be made with the same weight of peeled prawns instead of the crab.

SERVES 4

Preparation time 15 minutes

8 cherry tomatoes
2 tablespoons olive oil
2 small courgettes, thinly sliced
1 garlic clove, crushed
1 x 170g can white crabmeat, well drained
2 tablespoons full-fat crème fraîche or double cream
a good shake of Tabasco sauce
1-2 teaspoons Dijon mustard
juice of ½ lemon
a good tablespoon snipped fresh chives
salt and freshly ground black pepper
a few fresh basil leaves, chopped

GARNISH

2 tomatoes, skinned (see step 1), seeded and finely chopped
1 tablespoon balsamic vinegar
2 tablespoons olive oil
4 sprigs fresh basil

PREPARING AHEAD *These tians can be made up to a day ahead, but they must, of course, be kept in the fridge, covered with clingfilm.*

1 To skin the cherry tomatoes, plunge in boiling water for about 6 seconds, immediately plunge in cold water and peel off the skin. Set aside.

2 Heat the oil in a frying pan, add the courgette slices and fry over a high heat until golden brown on one side. Add the garlic, turn the courgette slices over, and continue to fry until brown. Set aside on kitchen paper to cool.

3 For the filling mix together the crabmeat, crème fraîche, Tabasco, mustard, lemon juice and chives, and season with salt and pepper.

4 Line a baking sheet with clingfilm and arrange four 7cm (3in) rings on top. Slice the skinned tomatoes (discarding the ends). Arrange the courgette and tomato slices alternately, about four of each, in the rings, then season and sprinkle with basil. Spoon the crab mixture into the rings and smooth the top. Arrange the remaining courgette and tomato slices on top of the crab mixture. Chill well before serving.

5 Lift the tians on to individual plates, and carefully remove the rings. Arrange the chopped tomato pieces around the plate. Mix the vinegar and oil in a small bowl and spoon at random over the tomatoes. Garnish with the sprigs of basil.

GOOD THINGS TO KNOW *Frozen white crabmeat is even better than canned, but it is very difficult to come by. Fresh white crabmeat is rarely sold without the dark meat, which is too wet to hold its shape in a tian.*

Smoked Haddock Florentine Pots

An uncomplicated yet impressive first course, which consists of individual ramekins containing fresh spinach, raw smoked haddock and a little cream, mustard and cheese sauce, which are baked. Serve them with really fresh rolls or bread. It's best to use a small spoon to eat them.

SERVES 6
Preparation time 10 minutes
Cooking time 15 minutes

300g (10oz) fresh spinach, washed
salt and freshly ground black
    pepper
freshly grated nutmeg
butter to grease
300g (10oz) undyed smoked
    haddock, skinned
150ml (¼ pint) double cream
1 teaspoon grainy mustard
45g (1 ½oz) mature Cheddar,
    grated
paprika

Preheat the oven to 220°C/
Fan 200°C/Gas 7.

PREPARING AHEAD *Bring everything together up to 12 hours ahead, and cook to serve.*

1 Wilt the spinach in a large saucepan without water, stirring frequently until it has all collapsed. Tip into a colander and squeeze out as much liquid as possible and dry off with kitchen paper until very dry.

2 Roughly chop the spinach and season with pepper and grated nutmeg. Divide between the bottom of six buttered ramekins. Arrange the ramekins on a baking tray.

3 Cut the smoked haddock into small chunks and arrange on the top of the spinach.

4 Mix the cream and mustard together and season with pepper and a little salt. Spoon over the fish and sprinkle with grated cheese.

5 Dust with paprika and bake in the preheated oven for about 12-15 minutes until bubbling and golden brown.

GOOD THINGS TO KNOW *There's no need to use baby spinach, use ordinary spinach or Swiss chard, and remove the stalks.*

AND ANOTHER THING *Baked haddock and egg makes a variation, which is good as a supper dish for 2–3. Spread the spinach across the base of a shallow ovenproof dish about 20 x 15cm (8 x 6in), cover with the haddock, and 3 hard-boiled eggs, quartered. Pour over the cream mixture, top with cheese and dust with paprika. Bake for about 20 minutes until the eggs are just set. To cook in the AGA, slide on to the second set of runners in the roasting oven for about 20 minutes.*

AGA To bake the ramekins, slide the baking sheet on to the top set of runners in the roasting oven for about 12-15 minutes.

Parma Ham with Mango and Mozzarella

A simple assembly of ingredients from a good supermarket: fresh mango, mozzarella cheese, with little pieces of dry-cured ham curled on top.

SERVES 4

Preparation time 10 minutes

50g (2oz) pine nuts
1 small mango
150g (5oz) mozzarella cheese
  (mozzarella di bufala)
1 x 85g bag watercress
8 slices Parma ham
balsamic vinegar
good extra virgin olive oil

PREPARING AHEAD *You could arrange the ingredients on individual platters about 3 hours in advance, covered with clingfilm, and kept in the fridge.*

1 Toast the pine nuts in a dry, non-stick pan over a medium heat for a few minutes until golden brown. Take great care as they can easily burn! Set aside.

2 Remove the flesh from either side of the flat mango stone (this runs through the centre of the mango). Peel then slice the flesh into fairly thin crescent shapes (any odd pieces can be served tucked under the mozzarella!).

3 Drain the mozzarella cheese and cut into thin slices.

4 Arrange the watercress in the centre of each plate. Divide the mango slices between the plates and arrange in a fan shape over the watercress. Top with the mozzarella slices then curl 2 pieces of ham on top of the mozzarella.

5 Sprinkle over the pine nuts and drizzle a little balsamic vinegar and oil around the plate.

GOOD THINGS TO KNOW *If you like to use toasted pine nuts fairly often, toast 200g (7oz) at a time very carefully in a dry, non-stick frying pan, stirring constantly. Watch like a hawk, as they burn very easily. Store surplus nuts in the freezer and just help yourself when you need them. Just warm them through first. They will keep in the freezer for up to two years, wrapped.*

Roasted Red Pepper and Goat's Cheese 'Chimneys' (V)

We just adore this recipe, which is perfect for a first course or light lunch. It consists of rolls of roasted peppers filled with mild goat's cheese and roasted aubergine, which are sliced just before serving, to be served cold with a dressed salad.

SERVES 6
Preparation time 10 minutes

1 x 375g jar red roasted peppers in oil (Tragano is good), or 6-9 large skinned peppers from the supermarket deli counter

1 x 150g tub soft mild goat's cheese (Chavroux)

salt and freshly ground black pepper

1 x 200g tub marinated grilled aubergine, or from the deli counter

a handful of fresh basil leaves, chopped

TO SERVE

a handful of lamb's lettuce leaves
a little French dressing

PREPARING AHEAD *The rolls can be stored, uncut, in the fridge overnight, where they will firm up beautifully. Cut and arrange just before serving.*

1 Remove the peppers from the jar. Arrange 6-9 peppers on a large chopping board or work top. Cut each pepper in half, remove seeds, and trim to about 10 x 13cm (4 x 5 in), saving any trimmings.

2 Spread each pepper half generously with goat's cheese and sprinkle with salt and pepper. Snip the aubergine into small pieces, then arrange a few pieces on each pepper, and sprinkle with a few basil leaves.

3 Roll up lengthways as tightly as possible with the join underneath (you may find it easy to roll the pepper on clingfilm as a guide). Wrap in clingfilm and chill in the fridge if time allows.

4 Cut each 'chimney-shaped' pepper in half diagonally. You may need to cut the ends to make the chimneys stand up.

5 Divide a little dressed lamb's lettuce between six plates and arrange 2-3 half peppers on each diagonally, cut-side uppermost.

GOOD THINGS TO KNOW *Red peppers are so much sweeter than the other coloured ones. Red peppers in oil from a jar are very good, but if you prefer you can roast your own (at 200°C/Fan 180°C/ Gas 6) then skin them and use the flesh. They can be tricky to peel, so once roasted and still hot, put into a poly bag and seal tightly – this will make them sweat. After about 20 minutes, the skin will peel off much more easily.*

AGA To roast raw peppers, arrange the halved peppers on a baking sheet, cut-side down, and slide on to the top set of runners in the roasting oven for about 35 minutes until the skins are bubbling and black. Skin as described above.

Mushroom and Aubergine Paté (V)

A good and simple first course, perfect for non-meat eaters, and any remainders make a tasty sandwich filling. Buy the aubergine from the deli counter in the supermarket.

SERVES 6
Preparation time 15 minutes

50g (2oz) butter, softened
1 small leek, finely sliced
1 small garlic clove, crushed
100g (4oz) chestnut mushrooms, sliced
225g (8oz) marinated and grilled aubergines, roughly chopped
150g (5oz) full-fat cream cheese
1 teaspoon lemon juice
25g (1oz) white breadcrumbs
salt and freshly ground black pepper
1 tablespoon chopped fresh parsley

PREPARING AHEAD *You can keep this, covered with clingfilm, in the fridge for up to a week.*

1 Melt half the butter in a large frying pan. Add the leek and garlic, and fry over a high heat for a couple of minutes. Cover and cook over a medium heat for about 10 minutes until just soft. Remove the lid, add the mushrooms and fry over a high heat for a few minutes, then stir in the aubergine and set aside to cool.

2 Spoon the mixture into a food processor with the remaining butter and the cheese, lemon juice and breadcrumbs. Whiz until smooth, then season to taste with salt and pepper.

3 Spoon into six ramekins or a terrine dish, scatter with parsley and chill before serving. Serve with toasted brown bread or Melba toast.

GOOD THINGS TO KNOW *Marinated grilled aubergine slices are also available in oil in jars. Once opened, keep in the fridge. They are delicious served with continental cold meats.*

Warm Smoked Chicken and Cherry Tomato Bruschetta

Smoked chicken comes in vacuum packs from good supermarkets. I have used cherry tomatoes on the vine as they look so attractive and keep their shape.

SERVES 4

Preparation time 10 minutes

12 cherry tomatoes on the vine,
    divided into 4 bunches of 3
100g (4oz) smoked chicken breast,
    sliced
1-2 tablespoons balsamic vinegar
a bunch of fresh watercress
2 tablespoons good olive oil

BRUSCHETTA

1 garlic clove, crushed
3 tablespoons olive oil
salt and freshly ground black
    pepper
1 thin French stick, cut into 8 thin
    slices on the diagonal

1 Preheat the grill to medium.

2 Mix the crushed garlic and oil together in a small bowl and season with salt and pepper. Brush both sides of the bread slices with the oil mixture.

3 Arrange the bread slices on a small foil-lined grill pan and toast under the grill on both sides for about 3-4 minutes until golden brown and crisp. Keep warm.

4 Brush the tomatoes with the remaining garlic oil and put on the same foil-lined grill pan. Slide under the grill for about 5 minutes or until just soft but still holding their shape.

5 Arrange the chicken slices on top of the tomatoes, drizzle over half the balsamic vinegar and return to the grill for a further couple of minutes to heat the chicken.

6 Take the end stalks off the watercress and discard. Arrange the waercress leaves on a plate, leaving a space for the bruschetta. Arrange two pieces of bruschetta in the centre of each plate, and divide the chicken evenly over them. Top with the bunches of tomatoes, and pour over the balsamic vinegar from the grill pan, along with the remaining vinegar. Sprinkle the olive oil over the watercress.

GOOD THINGS TO KNOW *Whole smoked chickens make a change from roasted chicken, and they are good for salads and sandwiches. Vacuum-packed thinly sliced chicken is ideal to wrap around tiny halved cherry tomatoes to serve with drinks.*

AGA Oven-fry the bread slices in the roasting oven and roast the tomatoes for about 3 minutes.

Fresh Figs with Parma Ham and Melon

Choose ripe figs. Avoid handling them too much, otherwise they will lose their cloudy bloom, like black grapes do. Home-grown figs in the summer are shiny, so there is no problem.

SERVES 4
Preparation time 10 minutes

1 ripe Cantaloupe melon
8 slices Parma ham
4 figs, halved lengthways through
  the stem

PREPARING AHEAD *You can prepare the plates a short time ahead, and keep them covered with clingfilm. If you want to do it well ahead, prepare the melon and figs, and add the ham later.*

1 Slice the melon in quarters lengthways. Remove the flesh from the skin by running your knife between the flesh and the skin, and chop the flesh into pieces. Divide the melon between four plates, making a pile in the centre of each plate.

2 Pile two pieces of ham on top of each pile of melon, curling the top with your fingers so it is piled high and not flat.

3 Put a fig half next to the melon on each plate. Cut the remaining halves halfway through the stem so they are still joined at the base, and open out slightly to form a 'V'.

4 Serve cold.

GOOD THINGS TO KNOW *To tell when melons are ripe, gently press the top at the opposite end to the stalk: if it is softish and smells ripe and sweet, it will be ripe. If buying a few days ahead, allow to ripen out of the fridge in a warm kitchen. Avoid blemished melons unless using for fruit salad and they are a bargain!*

Garlic Portabella Mushrooms with Bacon

Large whole mushrooms with a chopped mushroom and bacon topping and a garlic cream sauce, these make a popular first course. They are also very good served with steaks.

SERVES 4

Preparation time 10 minutes

100g (4oz) bacon lardons or
    streaky bacon, chopped
1 tablespoon olive oil
4 large Portabella mushrooms,
    stalks removed
300ml (½ pint) double cream
2 garlic cloves, crushed
250g (9oz) small chestnut
    mushrooms, quartered
salt and freshly ground black
    pepper
2 tablespoons chopped fresh
    parsley

PREPARING AHEAD *As the mushrooms are so fast to prepare and cook, it is best to make and cook them just before serving.*

1 Fry the bacon in a non-stick frying pan until golden brown and crisp, lift out and keep warm.

2 Heat the oil in the same pan and brown the Portabella mushrooms on both sides for a few minutes. Set aside and keep warm.

3 Add the double cream and garlic to the unwashed frying pan, and reduce over a high heat until thickened, stirring all the time.

4 Drop the chestnut mushrooms into the thickened cream and cook for a further 3-4 minutes. Season with salt and pepper.

5 Arrange a Portabella mushroom in the centre of each plate (gill-side up), and spoon over the cream mixture. Sprinkle with the bacon and parsley.

GOOD THINGS TO KNOW *Portabella mushrooms are large flat mushrooms, sometimes called field mushrooms. There is no need to peel off the outer skin, just wipe over the top.*

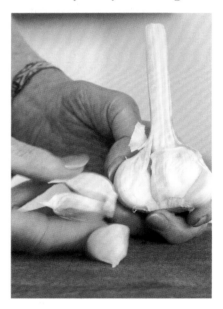

CHAPTER 3
MAIN COURSES
POULTRY AND GAME   BEEF, LAMB AND PORK   FISH

You may think it strange to include meat stews and things like moussaka in a book with the word 'fast' in the title. Many of these recipes, I must admit, take really quite a long time to cook, but once again, it's all in the planning. The great advantage of many of the recipes in this long chapter is that you can cook them well ahead of serving (or at least do a lot of the preparation ahead). This means that while the dish is simmering in the oven, you can be getting on with other things, as a stew doesn't need to be watched. On the evening of your party, when you are just reheating something you made the day before, you can be spending your precious time making a first course, or creating the finishing touches for a pudding. This is invaluable for people who are working during the day, and are busy. If you choose a dish that can be prepared ahead – some of them even need to be prepared ahead – you can make everything fit your own particular time scale.

The recipes have been conceived with all these ideas in mind. In the poultry and game section, most of the recipes use cuts of birds – such as breasts and thighs – as they are readily available now and are quicker to cook. In the past I always fried my chicken pieces before cooking them further in a sauce. Now, with the idea of speed in mind, I tend often to make my own 'cook-in' sauce, and simply drop the pieces of chicken into it to cook. If the sauce is well seasoned enough, its flavours will penetrate the meat during the brief cooking – and, most importantly, the whole dish will be less fatty, having not used any oil or butter. There are also some recipes here which use already cooked chicken (or turkey, of course); with a good sauce, these can be very useful when you are up against it so far as time is concerned. I'm very proud of my rabbit recipe here, the first time in any of my books. Rabbit is increasingly available, and it is delicious, well worth trying.

Good butchers and fishmongers seem to be rather thin on the ground now, but luckily our supermarkets have improved tremendously in both departments, and there is now a wide selection of meat and fish available. Most of the fish recipes here are already speedy in essence – as fish takes so little time to cook – and I use a few of the very good ready-prepared ingredients you can buy in jars and packets to enhance the flavours of fresh fish and shellfish. And in the quest for speed, you can freeze some meat and poultry dishes.

Chicken Saltimbocca with a hint of Mustard

A variation on the veal classic, but with added flavours – beaten-out chicken breasts spread with cheese and mustard, and topped with Parma ham. It's so quick to do, and thus is perfect for serving to family or friends for supper. You will need some wooden cocktail sticks.

SERVES 6

Preparation time 10 minutes
Cooking time 15 minutes

6 chicken breasts, boneless and
  skinless
100g (4oz) full-fat cream cheese
2 tablespoons grainy mustard
salt and freshly ground black
  pepper
6 thin slices Parma ham
12 large sage leaves
a little melted butter

SAUCE

150ml (¼ pint) white wine
1 tablespoon redcurrant jelly
50g (2oz) butter, cubed

Preheat the oven to 200°C/
Fan 180°C/Gas 6.

PREPARING AHEAD *These can be prepared the day ahead, and kept in the fridge, covered with clingfilm.*

1 Place the chicken breasts on a chopping board, cover with clingfilm, then bash each breast using a rolling pin until it has doubled in size and is flat and of an even thickness.

2 Mix the cheese with the mustard in a small bowl, and season with salt and pepper. Divide the mixture into six and spread over each flattened chicken breast, leaving a little gap around the edge. Place a piece of Parma ham on top of each breast, covering the cheese. Slice each breast in half lengthways. Arrange a sage leaf in the centre of each half on top of the Parma ham, and hold in place with a cocktail stick.

3 Arrange the chicken halves snugly in a buttered roasting tin and roast in the preheated oven for about 10-15 minutes or until the chicken is cooked and the ham is crisp. Remove the cocktail sticks, and keep the chicken warm while making the sauce. Take care not to overcook.

4 Put the roasting tin over a high heat on the hob and add the wine and redcurrant jelly. Reduce the sauce, whisking in the butter until the sauce thickens a little.

5 Season well, strain (don't worry about straining if you don't mind the bits!) and serve hot with the chicken.

6 To serve, arrange 2 chicken halves in a cross shape on each plate, and serve with a little sauce.

GOOD THINGS TO KNOW *Fresh sage, a wonderful herb, is available all year round in the supermarkets and is very easy to grow at home. It needs pruning after flowering, just above the old wood.*

AGA Slide on the second set of runners in the roasting oven for about 10 minutes until just cooked.

Fragrant Chicken

This recipe will be loved by many, as it is full of flavour with a subtle hint of curry. Serve with rice and poppadums if liked.

SERVES 6

Preparation time 10 minutes
Cooking time 15 minutes

6 chicken breasts, boneless and
  skinless
1 tablespoon runny honey
3 tablespoons sunflower oil
2 onions, very finely sliced
1 tablespoon curry powder
2 tablespoons brandy
300ml (½ pint) double cream
1 tablespoon mango chutney
juice of ½ lemon
salt and freshly ground black
  pepper
1 tablespoon chopped fresh
  parsley

PREPARING AHEAD *Takes no time at all, so prepare and cook just before serving.*

1. Slice the chicken into three strips lengthways and toss in the honey.

2. Heat 2 tablespoons of the oil in a large non-stick frying pan and brown the chicken strips all over (you may need to do this in batches). Set aside.

3. Heat the remaining oil in the unwashed pan, add the onions, and fry over a medium heat for about 10 minutes or until softened.

4. Sprinkle the curry powder over the onions, then add the brandy and stir. Mix in the double cream and return the chicken to the pan. Cover and simmer over a low heat for about 5 minutes or until the chicken is cooked through and the onions are soft.

5. Stir in the mango chutney and lemon juice and season well. Serve sprinkled with parsley.

GOOD THINGS TO KNOW *To get more juice out of lemons, quickly warm the lemons for about 30 seconds on full power in the microwave, then halve and squeeze out the juice.*

AGA Brown the chicken on the boiling plate. Start the onions on the boiling plate and then cover and cook in the simmering oven for about 10 minutes or until tender. Put the onions back on the boiling plate and add the other ingredients.

Spicy Chicken Wraps

These are tortilla wraps filled with a spicy chicken mixture, cooked with a simple tomato sauce.

SERVES 4

Preparation time 15 minutes
Cooking time 15 minutes

2 chicken breasts, boneless and
   skinless
1 tablespoon sunflower oil
salt and freshly ground black
   pepper
2 small green peppers, seeded
   and cut into 4cm (1 ½in) dice
1 large red onion, sliced
2 teaspoons ground cumin
2 teaspoons harissa paste
1 x 400g can chopped tomatoes
juice of 1 lime
4 tortilla wraps
finely grated zest of ½ lime
50g (2oz) Cheddar, grated

Preheat the oven to 200°C/
Fan 180°C/Gas 6. You will need
a 1.7 litre (3 pint) ovenproof dish.

PREPARING AHEAD *You could prepare the dish up to step 5 a day ahead of the final topping and baking.*

1 Cut the chicken breasts into long thin strips.

2 Heat the oil in a large non-stick frying pan. Season then brown the chicken strips all over. Remove with a slotted spoon and set aside.

3 Add the peppers and onion to the unwashed pan and fry for a minute. Sprinkle in the cumin and add 1 teaspoon of the harissa paste. Fry, stirring, for 5 minutes.

4 Return the chicken to the pan, add a third of the tomatoes and season well. Bring to the boil, then cover and simmer for about 5 minutes or until the peppers are soft and the chicken is cooked through.

5 Add the lime juice and stir well. Divide the mixture into four. Spoon each portion into the centre of each tortilla and roll tightly into a cigar shape. Arrange snugly in the dish.

6 Mix the remaining tomatoes with the lime zest and remaining harissa paste, and season well. Pour over the tortillas in the dish, and sprinkle with the cheese.

7 Bake in the preheated oven for about 15 minutes or until golden brown on top and hot in the centre.

GOOD THINGS TO KNOW *Harissa paste comes in a little jar and has a lovely flavour and quite a kick. You can make this dish extra spicy by adding an extra teaspoon of harissa paste to the chicken mixture.*

AGA Cook on the grid shelf on the floor of the roasting oven for about 10-15 minutes.

Turkey Korma

A very good hot way of using up the last cuts of the turkey at Christmas, but also excellent with chicken at any time of year. Ensure your turkey is still fresh off the carcass – not one that has been hanging around for days, in and out of the fridge. Serve with rice or naan bread, poppadums and mango chutney.

SERVES 6
Preparation time 20 minutes
Cooking time 15 minutes

450g (1lb) cooked turkey, cut into
  neat pieces

KORMA SAUCE
1-2 tablespoons sunflower oil
3 large onions, very roughly
  chopped
2 fat garlic cloves, crushed
1 teaspoon ground cardamom
5cm (2in) piece fresh root ginger,
  grated
1 tablespoon ground cumin
1 tablespoon ground coriander
1 tablespoon garam masala
300ml (½ pint) turkey or chicken
  stock
1 x 200ml carton coconut cream
  (UHT)
salt and freshly ground black
  pepper
50g (2oz) ground almonds

TO SERVE
150g (5oz) green seedless grapes,
  cut in half lengthways
2 tablespoons chopped fresh
  coriander or parsley

1 Heat a large frying pan, add the oil and onion, and fry over a high heat for a few minutes. Lower the heat, cover the pan and soften for about 20 minutes.

2 Add the garlic, cardamom, ginger, cumin, coriander and garam masala to the onion. Fry for a further few minutes over a high heat to draw out the flavouring oils from the spices.

3 Stir in the stock and coconut cream, bring to simmering point, season and stir in the ground almonds to thicken.

4 Add the cooked turkey to the hot sauce, and bring back to the boil. Cover and simmer over a low heat for about 15 minutes until the turkey is piping hot. Stir in the grapes and sprinkle over the chopped coriander.

GOOD THINGS TO KNOW *Most sauces such as korma sauce can be made well ahead and kept in the fridge for two or three days. They can then just be reheated and the cooked meat dropped into them and reheated for a further 15 minutes or so.*

AGA Start the onion on the boiling plate, then cover and transfer to the simmering oven for about 30 minutes. Continue as above on the boiling plate.

Mustard Chicken Normande

This is a very quick and delicious recipe, which has proved very popular at our workshops. I used to do this recipe with cider, but find that apple juice is far nicer and everyone is happy to drink what's left!

SERVES 6
Preparation time 20 minutes
Cooking time 20 minutes

1 tablespoon sunflower oil
6 small chicken breasts, boneless
   and skinless
1 large onion, thinly sliced
1 garlic clove, crushed
1 dessert apple, peeled, cored
   and coarsely grated
1 teaspoon redcurrant jelly
150ml (¼ pint) apple juice
2 tablespoons grainy mustard
400ml (14fl oz) full-fat crème
   fraîche
1 tablespoon cornflour, slaked in a
   little apple juice
salt and freshly ground black
   pepper
2 tablespoons chopped fresh
   parsley

PREPARING AHEAD *Make completely a day ahead, and reheat.*

1 Heat the oil in a large frying pan, and fry the chicken breasts over a high heat until brown all over. Remove with a slotted spoon and set aside.

2 Add the onion and garlic to the pan, and stir over a high heat for a few minutes. Cover and simmer for about 20 minutes until soft.

3 Add the apple, redcurrant jelly, apple juice and mustard to the onion, stirring, and bring to the boil. Spoon in the crème fraîche and slaked cornflour. Continue to stir until the sauce has thickened, then season with salt and pepper.

4 Return the chicken to the pan, cover with a lid, and bring to the boil. Simmer for about 15-20 minutes or until the chicken is just cooked.

5 Serve sprinkled with chopped parsley.

GOOD THINGS TO KNOW *Look out for smaller chicken breasts, as some are very large and too much for a single portion. They are now available with or without skin, so we have the choice. If you have any apple juice left and you don't want to drink it, freeze it in 150ml (¼ pint) pots and use it for this recipe at a future date.*

AGA Bring the chicken and sauce to the boil, cover and transfer to the simmering oven for about 30 minutes until the chicken is just done.

Claret Chicken with Thyme and Crispy Bacon

The great advantage of this recipe is that the sauce can be made well ahead, then just spooned over the marinated chicken breasts.

SERVES 6
Preparation time 20 minutes
Cooking time 30 minutes

6 small chicken breasts, boneless
    and skinless
2 tablespoons brandy
2 fat garlic cloves, crushed
225g (8oz) streaky bacon, cut into
    strips (or buy lardons)
1 large onion, sliced
250g (9oz) chestnut mushrooms,
    sliced
1 tablespoon sunflower oil
25g (1oz) butter
3 level tablespoons plain flour
300ml (½ pint) red wine
150ml (¼ pint) chicken stock
1 tablespoon each of tomato
    purée, soy sauce and
    redcurrant jelly
salt and freshly ground black
    pepper
1 tablespoon chopped fresh
    thyme
2 tablespoons chopped fresh
    parsley

Preheat the oven to 200°C/
Fan 180°C/Gas 6.

PREPARING AHEAD *Sauces (without cream) and gravies can be made up to two days ahead and kept in the fridge, or they can be frozen. The lardons can be made ahead and stored in the fridge.*

1 Put the chicken breasts into a poly bag and add the brandy and crushed garlic. Seal the top of the bag and massage the flavours into the chicken. Leave to marinate for as long as possible, overnight is ideal.

2 Fry the bacon in a large dry frying pan over a high heat until crisp, remove with a slotted spoon, drain on kitchen paper and set to one side.

3 Add the onion to any bacon fat in the pan, cook for 2-3 minutes over a high heat, then lower the heat, cover and cook for about 20 minutes until soft.

4 Remove the lid, turn up the heat, add the mushrooms and fry for 2-3 minutes, adding the oil and butter. Lower the heat, stir in the flour and slowly blend in the red wine and stock, stirring all the time. Bring to the boil, add the tomato purée, soy sauce, redcurrant jelly, seasoning and thyme, and boil for a few minutes. Set to one side until ready to cook the chicken breasts.

5 Arrange the chicken breasts in an ovenproof dish in a single layer. Pour the sauce over the chicken, cover with foil and cook in the preheated oven for about 20-30 minutes until the chicken is tender. Reheat the lardons, uncovered, in the oven for about 10 minutes.

6 Sprinkle the lardons and parsley over the chicken to serve.

GOOD THINGS TO KNOW *If time really is short, forget marinating the chicken, and add garlic and brandy to the sauce.*

AND ANOTHER THING *Fresh thyme is easy to grow in the garden or in a window box outside. It's simple to grow from seed, or buy a plant from the nursery. To take the leaves from the stem, pull the leaves back from the stem towards the root end.*

AGA Cook on the second set of runners in the roasting oven for about 20 minutes (see step 5).

Tarragon Chicken with White Grapes

A perfect chilled salad, good for a buffet. If time allows, mix the chicken and sauce the day ahead and chill, then add the avocado just before serving. Some people are not keen on anchovies, but don't be put off – I think they make all the difference.

SERVES 6

Preparation time 10 minutes, plus marinating time

1lb (450g) cooked chicken, boneless and skinless
3 spring onions, finely sliced

TARRAGON SAUCE
2 teaspoons Dijon mustard
3 tablespoons white wine vinegar
1 good tablespoon caster sugar
5 tablespoons sunflower oil
3 large anchovy fillets, drained of oil, finely chopped
200g (7oz) half-fat crème fraîche
1 tablespoon chopped fresh tarragon
1 tablespoon chopped fresh parsley
salt and freshly ground black pepper

TO SERVE
250g (9oz) large white seedless grapes, halved
a bunch of fresh watercress
2 spring onions, trimmed and cut into thin strips about 4cm (1 ½in) in length

PREPARING AHEAD *Do so totally the day before, but don't add the grapes until the last minute.*

1 Cut the chicken into bite-sized pieces and mix with the spring onions in a bowl.

2 Whisk all the sauce ingredients together in a bowl, taste and add a little more seasoning if needed.

3 Add the sauce to the chicken and mix well. Cover and marinate overnight in the fridge if time allows.

4 At the last minute add the white grapes to the salad, and spoon into a serving dish. Garnish with fresh watercress and fine slices of spring onions.

GOOD THINGS TO KNOW *Preserved salted anchovy fillets are packed in oil either in a small flat tin or a small jar. If you are only using a few anchovies, it's best to buy them in a jar so that the remainder can be used later. They keep for three weeks in the fridge: the oil will solidify, but will quickly go runny in a warm room.*

Pan-fried Paprika Chicken

I made a very similar dish to this on the BBC's **Saturday Kitchen,** *working with Antony Worrall Thompson. I used chicken breasts instead of thighs (which take less time in cooking), and added 150ml (¼ pint) cream to deglaze the pan instead of the water.*

SERVES 4-6
Preparation time 5 minutes, plus marinating time
Cooking time 10 minutes

6 chicken thighs, boneless and skinless
a little sunflower oil

MARINADE
2 tablespoons Worcestershire sauce
2 tablespoons runny honey
1 tablespoon paprika
1 tablespoon grainy mustard

PREPARING AHEAD *The chicken can be beaten out and marinated up to 8 hours ahead.*

1 Cut each thigh open and flatten out by covering with a piece of clingfilm and banging out evenly with a rolling pin to about 2.5cm (1in).

2 Measure the marinade ingredients together into a large bowl and mix well. Add the chicken thighs to the marinade, cover and leave for about 15 minutes or as long as time allows.

3 Heat a large non-stick frying pan until very hot. Remove the chicken from the marinade, keeping the liquid, and brush the thighs with a little oil.

4 Fry the chicken thighs gently for about 3-5 minutes on each side until dark golden brown and cooked through. Lift the chicken out of the pan into a serving dish and set aside.

5 Pour the marinade into the same pan along with 6 tablespoons water. Bubble over a high heat, then spoon over the chicken and serve.

GOOD THINGS TO KNOW *In summer cook the chicken on the barbecue and serve without the juices (or boil juices in a pan on the barbecue). If you like skin on your chicken, leave it on, but do be careful to trim off any surplus.*

AND ANOTHER THING *This doesn't make a large amount of sauce – double the quantities if you like a lot.*

Thai Shiitake Chicken

One of those wonderful prepare-ahead main courses. The chicken breasts are carved into pieces before the final cooking so that those that want less can take just a couple of slices – and the chicken does not need to be pre-fried.

SERVES 6

Preparation time 10 minutes
Cooking time 30 minutes

1 tablespoon sunflower oil
300g (10oz) shiitake mushrooms, sliced
salt and freshly ground black pepper
1 tablespoon red Thai curry paste
1 tablespoon tamarind paste
1 x 400ml can coconut milk
1 teaspoon fish sauce
juice and finely grated zest of 2 limes
2 teaspoons caster sugar
1 tablespoon cornflour, slaked with a little coconut milk
6 chicken breasts, boneless and skinless
a bunch of fresh basil or coriander, chopped

Preheat the oven to 200°C/ Fan 180°C/Gas 6.

PREPARING AHEAD *Arrange the mushrooms and chicken in the serving dish, but do not pour the sauce over until just before cooking. Bring the sauce back to the boil before pouring over the chicken. There is plenty of sauce, enough for 8-10 chicken breasts, so you could serve any left over the next day with prawns.*

1 Heat the oil in a large non-stick frying pan, add the mushrooms and fry over a high heat for a few minutes. Season with salt and pepper and arrange over the base of a large shallow ovenproof dish.

2 To the unwashed pan, add the Thai paste, tamarind paste, coconut milk, fish sauce, lime juice and zest, and sugar. Bring to the boil and boil for a few minutes. Season.

3 Add a little hot sauce to the slaked cornflour and tip into the pan with the sauce, stirring continually while bringing back to the boil. The sauce will thicken.

4 Cut each chicken breast into three widthways, then reassemble and lie on top of the mushrooms. Pour over the boiling hot Thai sauce and bake immediately in the preheated oven for about 20-30 minutes.

5 Sprinkle with chopped basil or coriander, and serve hot.

GOOD THINGS TO KNOW *This dish may be made with pheasant breasts, but take care not to overcook. Tamarind paste is bought in jars from good supermarkets – it is a purée of tamarind (a sour tree fruit), which is used in curries and some hot chutneys.*

AGA Slide on to the second set of runners in the roasting oven for about 20-30 minutes.

Five-spice Mango Chicken

This is perfect to serve cold for a buffet or when cooking for numbers, as it is so light and fresh – and there is not a drop of mayonnaise in sight! It can be made a day ahead and kept in the fridge, which gives time for the flavours to really infuse into the chicken.

SERVES 8-10

Preparation time 15 minutes

750g (1 ¾lb) fresh cooked chicken meat, without bone

salt and freshly ground black pepper

MANGO SAUCE

2 large mangoes, peeled

8 mild peppadew peppers from a jar

6 tablespoons mango chutney

1 x 200ml carton Greek yoghurt

1 tablespoon Chinese five-spice powder

juice of 1 lemon

a few drops of Tabasco sauce

GARNISH

fresh salad leaves

2 mild peppadew peppers, thinly sliced

lots of chopped fresh parsley

PREPARING AHEAD *If you want to make this a day ahead, omit adding the chopped mango and leave it mixed with a little lemon juice in a bowl in the fridge. Just stir in before serving.*

1 For the sauce, cut the flesh of 1 mango roughly into pieces and put in a food processor. Add the rest of the ingredients, and whiz until smooth and blended. Season with salt and pepper.

2 Cut the chicken into neat pieces and mix with the mango sauce in a mixing bowl. Cut the flesh of the remaining mango into 1cm (½in) pieces and mix in with the chicken mixture. Taste and check the seasoning.

3 Spoon the chicken mixture into a dish, decorate with a few salad leaves, and sprinkle over the peppadew slices and parsley. Serve cold.

GOOD THINGS TO KNOW *To serve hot (I really was surprised this worked so well!), simply add 1 tablespoon cornflour to the mango mixture before blending in the processor. Then add the chicken and mango, pile into a shallow ovenproof dish, and bake at 200ºC/Fan 180ºC/Gas 6 for about 15 minutes until very hot. Sprinkle with peppadew slices and serve.*

AGA To serve hot, slide on to the second set of runners in the roasting oven for about 15 minutes until very hot. Sprinkle with peppadew slices and serve.

Coconut and Lime Chicken

I think the thigh is the best part of the chicken and, unlike the breast, it does not matter if you slightly overcook it because the meat is more succulent (this makes it perfect for the barbecue too). Runny honey is easiest, but use what you have in the cupboard.

SERVES 4

Preparation time 5 minutes, plus marinating time
Cooking time 20 minutes

8 chicken thighs, boneless and
 skinless
2 tablespoons sunflower oil

MARINADE

1 x 200ml carton coconut cream
 (UHT)
2 tablespoons runny honey
3 tablespoons Thai red curry paste
juice and finely grated zest of 2
 limes
salt and freshly ground black
 pepper

PREPARING AHEAD

Marinate the thighs a day ahead.

1 Whisk together the marinade ingredients in a bowl until combined, then season well.

2 Toss the chicken thighs in the marinade so they are evenly coated. Cover the bowl with clingfilm and leave in the fridge overnight or, if time is short, for a minimum of 30 minutes.

3 Remove the chicken thighs from the marinade. Preheat a large non-stick frying pan until very hot. Add the oil and brown the chicken thighs for about 3 minutes on each side until golden brown. Lower the heat, cover, and cook through, another 10-15 minutes. (You may need to do this in batches, and it may take a little longer.) Arrange in a serving dish.

4 Pour the marinade into the same frying pan, bring to the boil and reduce for a minute or so to thicken slightly. Pour over the cooked chicken thighs to serve.

5 Serve hot with lime wedges, rice and prawn crackers.

GOOD THINGS TO KNOW *Coconut cream is UHT, creamy and thick and comes in a carton. Do not get this muddled with coconut milk which is in a can; this is much thinner and would be too thin for this recipe.*

AGA Cook the chicken thighs on the boiling plate for 3 minutes on each side, then transfer to the simmering oven for a further 20 minutes, or until tender.

Aromatic Spiced Duck

If you don't want to skin the duck breasts, cook the skin side more slowly to get the skin crispy (about 15 minutes) and let the fat run out.

SERVES 4
Preparation time 10 minutes
Cooking time 8 minutes

25g (1oz) soft butter
4 large duck breasts, skinless and
  boneless
salt and freshly ground black
  pepper
2.5cm (1in) piece fresh root ginger,
  finely grated
1 teaspoon Chinese five-spice
  powder
4 tablespoons plum sauce
225ml (8fl oz) orange juice

TO SERVE
slices of fresh orange
lots of fresh watercress

PREPARING AHEAD *If the duck breasts didn't come unskinned, skin them in advance as it takes time.*

1 Heat a non-stick frying pan until very hot.

2 Spread half of the butter over the duck breasts and season with salt and pepper.

3 Fry the duck breasts for about 3 minutes on each side (for pink in the middle), transfer to a plate, cover with foil and keep warm while making the sauce.

4 Heat the remaining butter in the unwashed frying pan, add the ginger and five-spice powder and fry for a minute over a high heat, before stirring in the remaining ingredients. Boil for a few minutes until the sauce has thickened a little. Season with salt and pepper.

5 To serve, slice the duck and arrange on a plate. Decorate with slices of orange and watercress, and serve with the sauce.

GOOD THINGS TO KNOW *Chicken breasts can be used instead if liked, but cook for a little longer until cooked right through.*

Highland Pheasant Casserole with Apples

If you haven't game stock, use chicken stock cubes. For a special occasion, prepare a few more apple wedges and fry in butter. Serve alongside the pheasant as a garnish.

SERVES 6
Preparation time 10 minutes
Cooking time 30 minutes

25g (1oz) butter
2 tablespoons sunflower oil
salt and freshly ground black
    pepper
6 pheasant breasts, skinned
2 onions, thinly sliced
25g (1oz) plain flour
150ml (¼ pint) apple juice
300ml (½ pint) game stock
2 dessert apples, peeled and cut
    into thin wedges
2 tablespoons double cream
1 tablespoon lemon juice

PREPARING AHEAD

Cook a day ahead, slightly undercooking, then reheat gently until hot.

1 Heat half the butter and all the oil in a large non-stick frying pan until very hot.

2 Season the pheasant breasts, and brown them in the hot frying pan over a high heat until brown, about 1-2 minutes on each side. Set aside.

3 Heat the remaining butter in the unwashed frying pan, add the onions and fry until they are tender and their wetness has evaporated, about 10-15 minutes.

4 Sprinkle in the flour and gradually blend in the apple juice and stock. Bring to the boil, stirring, then add the apples and pheasant breasts, and season with salt and pepper. Cover and simmer over a low heat for about 12 minutes or until the pheasant breasts are just cooked through. Do not overcook.

5 Stir in the double cream and lemon juice, check the seasoning and serve hot.

GOOD THINGS TO KNOW

Pheasant legs are not suitable for this recipe as the cooking time is very short and legs need long slow cooking otherwise they are tough.

AGA Bring to the boil after seasoning in step 4, cover and transfer to the simmering oven for about 15 minutes until the breasts are just cooked.

Roast Partridge with Pancetta

If the birds are large, you want to serve half only per person – in which case you will need to double the rest of the ingredients in order to serve more people. Carve in half after roasting. If you wish, serve bread sauce with the birds, and for a fruit jelly use redcurrant or apple.

SERVES 4
Preparation time 5 minutes
Cooking time 20 minutes

4 small knobs butter
4 sprigs fresh rosemary
salt and freshly ground black
  pepper
4 partridges, English if you can get
  them
4 rashers pancetta
2 slices bread, cut in half, crusts
  removed
sunflower oil

GRAVY

1 tablespoon cornflour
2 tablespoons sherry
300ml (½ pint) game or chicken
  stock
a dash of balsamic vinegar

Preheat the oven to 200°C/
Fan 180°C/Gas 6.

PREPARING AHEAD *Make the gravy ahead, then add the juices from the roasted birds at the last minute.*

1 Put a knob of butter, a sprig of rosemary and some seasoning in the cavity of each bird. Cover the breasts of each bird with a slice of pancetta.

2 Roast in the preheated oven for about 20 minutes, or about 15 if the birds are very small. Then cover, rest and keep warm.

3 Fry the slices of bread on both sides in a little sunflower oil until crisp. Drain well on kitchen paper.

4 To make the gravy, blend the cornflour and sherry together until smooth. Pour the sherry and cornflour into the stock, bring to the boil, stirring all the time, and add any juices from the roasting tin. Add the balsamic vinegar and season well.

5 Serve each bird on the crispy bread with the hot gravy.

GOOD THINGS TO KNOW *Partridges are in season from 1st September to 1st February and are now more plentiful as, like pheasants, they are bred for the shoot. Pancetta is an Italian dry-cured bacon.*

AGA Slide on to the top set of runners in the roasting oven for about 15 minutes until cooked through. Rest before serving.

Rabbit Casserole with Port and Mushrooms

A wonderful way of cooking young rabbit or skinned chicken thighs. If the rabbit is older, the cooking time will be much longer. Serve with creamy mash and buttered cabbage or green beans.

SERVES 4-6

Preparation time 10 minutes
Cooking time 1 ¼ hours

2 young rabbits, jointed
50g (2oz) plain flour
salt and freshly ground black pepper
about 75g (3oz) butter
1 tablespoon sunflower oil
12 shallots or pickling onions
900ml (1 ½ pints) hot game or beef stock
150ml (¼ pint) port
1 good tablespoon redcurrant jelly
1 tablespoon balsamic vinegar
¼ teaspoon Tabasco sauce
350g (12oz) small chestnut mushrooms, halved
3 sprigs fresh thyme
plenty of chopped fresh parsley

Preheat the oven to 160°C/
Fan 140°C/Gas 3.

PREPARING AHEAD *This can be made up to two days ahead and reheated. It freezes well too, but best to add the mushrooms as it is reheated.*

1 Toss the rabbit joints in seasoned flour. Put 25g (1oz) of the butter and all the oil into a large non-stick frying pan and fry the joints until golden brown (you may need to do this in batches). Lift out into a flameproof casserole.

2 In the same pan, fry the whole shallots, adding a little more oil if necessary. When golden brown, lift out and set aside with the rabbit.

3 Add the seasoned flour to the unwashed frying pan, and stir well to form a roux. Slowly blend in half of the stock, and allow to thicken, stirring all the time. Add the remaining stock, along with the port, redcurrant jelly, balsamic vinegar and Tabasco. Season with salt and pepper.

4 Pour over the rabbit and shallots, add the mushrooms and thyme, and bring to the boil. Cover with a lid, transfer to the preheated oven, and cook for about an hour until the rabbit is tender.

5 To serve, check the seasoning and remove the thyme sprigs. Leave the joints whole except for the back (the saddle). I find it best to take a sharp knife and cut the two fillets either side of the back off and discard the bones. This will give you four strips from both backs. Return them to the casserole, and sprinkle generously with parsley.

GOOD THINGS TO KNOW *If time is short, use 2 large onions, roughly chopped, instead of shallots or pickling onions, as the latter can be fiddly to peel.*

AND ANOTHER THING *Each skinned young rabbit is usually cut into five pieces, the back (saddle) and four leg joints. Buy from your butcher, farmers' market or a good supermarket.*

AGA Bring to the boil on the boiling plate, cover and transfer to the simmering oven for about 1-2 hours, or until tender.

Char-grilled Steaks with Onion Marmalade and Asparagus

If you don't have time to make your own onion marmalade, buy a jar – the bought ones are very good. You will not need all the marmalade in this recipe, but it keeps well in the fridge for up to a week, or it freezes well too.

SERVES 4
Preparation time 15 minutes, plus marmalade time
Cooking time 5 minutes

4 fillet steaks, about 175g (6oz) each, cut from the thick end
a little soft butter
salt and freshly ground black pepper
100g (4oz) or 12 asparagus tips, cooked until just done, 3-4 minutes
25g (1oz) fresh Parmesan shavings
paprika

ONION MARMALADE
1 tablespoon olive oil
2 large Spanish onions, thinly sliced
1 teaspoon caster sugar
1 good teaspoon balsamic vinegar

CHEAT'S AÏOLI
2 tablespoons crème fraîche
4 tablespoons low-fat mayonnaise
2 garlic cloves, crushed
chopped fresh tarragon, to taste

PREPARING AHEAD *Fry the fillet steaks exactly as in the recipe. Top them with onion marmalade, asparagus etc. Lift on to a baking tray, cover with clingfilm and chill. To reheat, remove the clingfilm and slide into a preheated oven at 220°C/ Fan 200°C/Gas 7 for about 7 minutes. Serve at once.*

1 Heat the oil for the onion marmalade in a large frying pan, add the onions and fry for a few minutes over a high heat. Add the sugar and some salt and pepper, cover and cook over a low heat until very soft, about an hour. Remove the lid and cook over a high heat for a few minutes to drive off any moisture, then add the vinegar and check the seasoning. Remove from the heat.

2 Mix all the aïoli ingredients together.

3 Heat a ridged grill pan over a high heat until very hot. Spread the steak with soft butter on one side and season with salt and pepper.

4 Add the steaks, buttered-side down, to the hot ridged grill pan, and fry over a high heat for 2 minutes on each side for medium rare. Arrange on a foil-lined grill pan.

5 Spoon a little onion marmalade on to each steak, and decorate with three asparagus tips. Sprinkle with Parmesan and paprika, and blast under a hot grill for a couple of minutes until hot. Serve with the aïoli.

GOOD THINGS TO KNOW

Instead of fillet steak you can use rib-eye steak, which is less expensive. It is cut from the sirloin end of the fore-rib and is full of flavour but not as tender as fillet. I find it works better to buy 2 thicker rib-eye steaks and cut them in half rather than buying 4 thin steaks which can dry out quite quickly.

AGA To prepare ahead, fry on boiling plate as in the recipe. Top with onion and asparagus etc. Lift on to a baking sheet, cover with clingfilm and chill. To reheat, remove the clingfilm and slide the sheet on to the top set of runners in the roasting oven for about 7 minutes. Serve at once.

How Do You Like Your Steak?

General Notes for Success

Choose top-quality steaks. In my opinion fillet steaks are the finest, closely followed by rib-eye, rump and sirloin. Fillet steaks were used in the photographs. The cooking time for other cuts of steak will be the same if they are the same thickness, while thinner steaks take less time, so adjust accordingly. Steaks can often be tough if overcooked, so always cook very carefully.

- Best to use a non-stick ridged grill pan or frying pan.
- Always have a very hot pan to start with.
- Oil or butter the steaks and not the pan. I like to season my steaks with ground black pepper and a little salt.
- Do not move the steaks around when they are frying. Only move when turning over.
- Always rest steaks before serving so the juices are re-absorbed. This allows the steak to stay moist, and prevents the juices running when carved. Note that the steaks will carry on cooking a little when resting.

DEGREES OF DONENESS

Illustrated are three 3cm (1¼in) thick, classically cut, really thick fillet steaks, weighing 175g (6oz) each. (As a family we often have the same weight of steak, cut to 2.5cm (1in) thick, and for medium-rare I cook them for 2 minutes on each side, and rest.)

Rare Heat a non-stick ridged grill pan until very hot. Spread a little softened butter or oil over the steaks and season with pepper and a little salt. Fry the steaks for 2 minutes on each side on a high heat, transfer to a warm plate and cover loosely with foil. Rest for about 5 minutes. The steaks should feel soft and springy to the touch, and be red in the middle.

Medium-rare Heat a non-stick ridged grill pan until very hot. Spread a little softened butter or oil over the steaks and season with pepper and a little salt. Fry the steaks for 3 minutes on each side over a high heat, transfer to a warm plate and loosely cover with foil. Rest for 5 minutes. The steaks should feel firm to the touch, and be pink in the middle.

Well-done Heat a non-stick ridged grill pan until very hot. Spread a little softened butter or oil over the steaks and season with pepper and a little salt. Fry the steaks for 3 minutes on each side over a high heat. Lower the heat to medium and fry for a further 3 minutes or so, depending on how well-done you want them. Transfer to a warm plate and loosely cover with foil. Rest for 5 minutes. The steak should feel very firm to the touch, and be grey in the middle.

| Rare | Medium rare | Well done |

Roast Fillet of Beef with Horseradish and Peppadew Sauce

A great luxury and very easy to prepare for a special occasion. If you want to cook a smaller fillet for fewer people, the timing will be only slightly less.

SERVES 8-12
Preparation time 5 minutes
Cooking time up to 30 minutes, depending on how well done you like it

1.4kg (3lb) whole fillet of beef cut from the centre
2 tablespoons olive oil
salt and freshly ground black pepper
a little butter

SAUCE
150ml (¼ pint) double cream
3 tablespoons creamed horseradish sauce
5 peppadew peppers, thinly sliced

Preheat the oven to 220°C/ Fan 200°C/Gas 7.

PREPARING AHEAD *Brown the meat up to a day ahead if it suits you (see step 3), and chill it, then all you have to do is bring it to room temperature and roast, for 30 minutes. The sauce can be made the day before as well.*

1 Rub the oil over the meat, and then season.

2 Heat a non-stick frying pan over high heat until very hot and brown the beef on all sides.

3 Transfer the fillet to a small roasting tin, spread with a little butter and roast in the preheated oven for about 30 minutes for medium rare (10 minutes per 450g/1lb). Leave to rest covered with foil for about 10 minutes. If the browned fillet is roasted straightaway, whilst still hot, it will only take 25 minutes; if left to go cold, you will need to roast for 30 minutes (see below). If your fillet is long and thin it will only take about 20 minutes.

4 Lightly whip the cream, stir in the horseradish and peppadew peppers, and season.

5 Thinly carve the beef and serve with the cold sauce.

GOOD THINGS TO KNOW *To serve leftover cooked fillet steak cold, leave it in the piece, then slice just before it is needed and it will still be beautifully pink. If you slice it ahead, the meat surface will turn grey half an hour or so after being exposed to the air. And if you like a stronger flavoured sauce, add hot horseradish sauce instead of creamed horseradish sauce to the cream, as well as a tablespoon of grainy mustard.*

AND ANOTHER THING *The cold cream sauce is perfect on its own, but you might get nagged to make a gravy. Rest the beef once cooked. Add a little more butter to the roasting tin, heat on the hob then add a tablespoon of plain flour. Blend with a whisk, then add about 300ml (½ pint) beef stock, still whisking well. Add 50ml (2fl oz) red wine if you've got it, a teaspoon of redcurrant jelly and a dash of Worcestershire sauce.*

AGA Roast on the second set of runners in the roasting oven for the same timings as in step 3.

Steak and Kidney Pie with Port and Pickled Walnuts

There is plenty of gravy so keep some back from the pie and serve it separately. You may well think this isn't quick, and it does take time to make, but it is marvellous to make completely ahead. It's great for a family gathering.

SERVES 8

Preparation time 20 minutes
Cooking time 3 hours 40 minutes

about 2 tablespoons sunflower oil
1.5kg (3 ¼lb) skirt beef, or good
    stewing steak, cut into 4cm
    (1 ½in) cubes
500g (1lb 2oz) ox kidney, trimmed
    and cut into 4cm (1 ½in) pieces
2 large onions, roughly chopped
75g (3oz) butter
75g (3oz) plain flour
900ml (1 ½ pints) beef stock
150ml (¼ pint) port
2-3 tablespoons Worcestershire
    sauce
2 tablespoons redcurrant jelly
salt and freshly ground black
    pepper
250g (9 oz) button mushrooms, left
    whole
1 x 390g jar pickled walnuts,
    drained and walnuts halved
500g (1 lb 2oz) puff pastry
1 egg, beaten

You will need a pie dish with a lip, of about 33 x 26 x 6cm (13 x 10 ½ x 2 ½in), with a capacity of 2.2 litres (4 pints). When ready to cook the whole pie, which is possibly a day after you have started, preheat the oven to 220°C/Fan 200°C/Gas 7.

1 Heat a little oil in a casserole and fry the beef and kidney cubes until brown all over (you may need to do this in batches). Lift out on to a plate using a slotted spoon, and set aside.

2 Heat a little more oil in the unwashed casserole, add the onion and fry for a few minutes over a high heat. Stir in the butter and melt, then blend in the flour, followed by the beef stock and port. Blend well, stirring all the time, until thickened, then add the Worcestershire sauce and redcurrant jelly.

3 Return the meat to the casserole and season with salt and pepper. Bring up to the boil, cover and simmer for about 3 hours or until the beef is tender.

4 Half an hour before the meat is ready, stir in the mushrooms and pickled walnuts. Taste for seasoning, then arrange the meat in the pie dish. Pour over most of the gravy so the dish is filled nearly up to the top, and reserve the remaining gravy to serve separately. Place an inverted handle-less cup or pie funnel into the centre of the dish (with the meat all around).

5 Set aside to cool in the fridge overnight or as long as possible so the filling sets.

6 Roll out the pastry on a lightly floured surface to the same shape as the dish but about 5cm (2in) wider all the way round. Cut strips from around the pastry about 2.5cm (1in) wide to use on top of the lip of the pie dish. Wet the lip on the dish, lay the thin strips of pastry on top, and brush with beaten egg. Carefully lift the rolled pastry on top of the dish and push down the edges so they stick to the pastry on the lip. Trim off any

excess pastry and flute the edges. Glaze with beaten egg. Cut out shapes from the pastry trimmings, and use to decorate the top, glazing these with egg as well.

7 Bake in the centre of the preheated oven for about 30-40 minutes, turning around halfway through, cooking until the meat bubbles. If the pastry is getting too brown, cover loosely with foil.

8 Serve with the remaining gravy, heated through, thinning it down with water if necessary.

GOOD THINGS TO KNOW *If you don't like pickled walnuts, just leave them out.*

AGA Bring the steak and kidney to the boil on the boiling plate. Put the lid on, and transfer to the simmering oven until tender, about 3 hours. Cool as above and continue with step 6. Bake the pie on the lowest set of runners in the roasting oven for about 30-40 minutes, turning around halfway through, until the meat is piping hot and the pastry is golden brown.

Beef Stroganoff

A modern version of the classic recipe, using the thin end of fillet steak, is cheaper and just as good as the thick end that is used for steaks. Traditionally ordinary button mushrooms are used, but chestnut mushrooms have a firmer texture and greater depth of flavour. If you can't get soured cream use full-fat crème fraîche.

SERVES 6

Preparation time 10 minutes
Cooking time 30 minutes

750g (1 ¾lb) tail end of fillet steak
salt and freshly ground black
    pepper
25g (1oz) butter
2 onions, finely sliced
about 3 tablespoons sunflower oil
1 tablespoon paprika
400g (14oz) button chestnut
    mushrooms, halved
1 x 284ml carton soured cream
juice of ½ lemon
2 tablespoons chopped fresh
    parsley

1 Cut the steak into thin strips on the slant, about 1 x 5cm (½ x 2in). Season the meat with salt and pepper.

2 Measure the butter into the pan, add the onions, cover and cook over a low heat until the onions are really tender, about 20 minutes.

3 Heat a large non-stick frying pan until hot, heat a little oil, and then add half the meat. Stir-fry really briskly for about a minute until brown but still pink in the centre. Lift out with a slotted spoon on to a plate. Add a little more oil to the pan if necessary and repeat the process with the rest of the steak – if cooked really fast there should be no juices left in the pan. Transfer when brown to the plate with the rest of the cooked steak. Take care not to overcook.

4 Remove the lid from the onions, and stir in the paprika and mushrooms. Turn up the heat and toss for a minute, then pour in any juices from the steak plate and cook to evaporate (as the beef stands, some juices will have seeped out).

5 Add the meat to the pan with the cream, and allow to just bubble to heat through. Add the lemon juice and seasoning, and cook over a low heat for a couple of minutes until the meat is just heated through.

6 Serve at once, with boiled rice or mashed potato, garnished with the parsley.

GOOD THINGS TO KNOW *You could also use trimmed rump steak for Stroganoff, but it isn't quite as tender and will need a slightly longer cooking time.*

Moussaka at its Best

A modern moussaka. There is no frying of the aubergine slices first, as blanching is healthier. And there's no classic white sauce to make, as we use Greek yoghurt with flour.

SERVES 8
Preparation time 15 minutes
Cooking time 2 ¾ hours

900g (2lb) raw minced lamb
2 large onions, roughly chopped
a little sunflower oil
2 fat garlic cloves, crushed
2 level tablespoons plain flour
2 x 400g cans chopped tomatoes
4 tablespoons tomato purée
salt and freshly ground black pepper
3 aubergines, sliced into 2cm (¾in) slices
4 good tablespoons chopped fresh mint

TOPPING
2 level tablespoons cornflour
1 x 500g tub Greek yoghurt
2 eggs
1 teaspoon Dijon mustard
75g (3oz) Parmesan, freshly grated

Preheat the oven to 200°C/ Fan 180°C/Gas 6. You will need a large ovenproof dish about 34 x 24cm (13 ½ x 9 ½in).

PREPARING AHEAD *This can be made completely and kept in the fridge for up to two days ahead. It freezes well too.*

1 Heat a large non-stick frying pan, add the mince and, using a wooden spoon, break up the lamb as it browns (you may need to do this in batches). Spoon the browned mince into a colander to drain off the fat.

2 Add the onions to the unwashed pan with a little oil and cook over a high heat for a few minutes. Return the lamb to the pan, add the garlic and blend in the flour. Add the tomatoes, tomato purée and some salt and pepper and stir well. Bring to the boil, allow to thicken, then cover and simmer over a low heat for about 2 hours until the meat is tender.

3 Blanch the aubergine in boiling salted water for about 5 minutes until just tender. Drain, first in a colander and then on kitchen paper.

4 For the topping, measure the cornflour into a bowl, blend in a little yoghurt, stir in the eggs and whisk until smooth. Mix in the remaining yoghurt and the mustard.

5 To assemble the moussaka, mix the mint with the mince. Spread half the meat mixture over the bottom of the ovenproof dish. Cover with half the aubergines, season, and repeat with the remaining meat and aubergine. Spread the yoghurt sauce over the top and sprinkle with the Parmesan cheese.

6 Cook in the preheated oven for about 45 minutes until the top is brown and bubbling.

GOOD THINGS TO KNOW *This recipe is not exactly quick, I know it takes time for the mince to become tender, but the important thing is that you don't have to be there, so you can be getting on with other things.*

AGA After step 2, bring to the boil on the boiling plate, cover and transfer to the simmering oven for about 2 hours. Continue with the rest of the recipe and cook the complete dish on the second set of runners in the roasting oven for about 45 minutes until golden brown.

A Lighter Irish Stew

For a traditional Irish stew, middle neck and scrag end of neck of lamb are used. Carrot is usually not added and sometimes pearl barley is included. This updated easy version uses neck fillet of lamb plus celeriac and carrots – a completely delicious comfort stew.

SERVES 6-8
Preparation time 15 minutes
Cooking time about 1 ½ hours

700g (1 ½lb) potatoes, sliced
450g (1lb) celeriac, peeled and
　thinly sliced
450g (1lb) carrots, peeled and
　thinly sliced
2 large onions, sliced
salt and freshly ground black
　pepper
700g (1 ½lb) lamb neck fillet, cut
　into 5cm (2in) pieces
5 fresh thyme sprigs
a bunch of fresh parsley, chopped

Preheat the oven to 160°C/
Fan 140°C/Gas 3.

PREPARING AHEAD *The preparation time is fast, with no sauces to make, and no thickening to do, but the cooking time is long, so choose to make it on a day when this fits in with your schedule.*

1 Arrange half the potatoes, celeriac, carrots and onions in a deep, flameproof casserole dish. Season with salt and pepper.

2 Place the lamb and thyme sprigs on top and season well.

3 Layer the remaining vegetables on top of the lamb, making sure the potatoes are the final layer on top.

4 Pour in enough water so the dish is half full, cover with a lid, and bring to the boil over a high heat. Transfer to the preheated oven, and cook for about an hour or until the lamb is just tender.

5 Increase the oven temperature to 200°C/Fan 180°C/ Gas 6, remove the lid and continue to cook for a further 25 minutes to allow the potatoes to brown.

6 Pull out the thyme sprigs as you are serving. Pour into soup bowls and sprinkle with chopped parsley.

GOOD THINGS TO KNOW *Celeriac has a really thick skin and needs to be peeled thickly and sliced just before cooking otherwise it will quickly discolour. Celeriac is not available in early summer, so add 6 sliced celery sticks instead.*

AGA At step 4, bring to the boil on the boiling plate, cover and transfer to the simmering oven for about 1 ½ hours or until tender. Remove the lid and move to the top of the roasting oven to brown for about 15 minutes.

Minted Lamb Steaks with Spring Vegetables

Cooking in individual parcels means no washing of pans after the meal, and the juices are kept in the parcels to pour over the lamb at the end.

SERVES 4
Preparation time 10 minutes
Cooking time 20 minutes

a little olive oil
4 lamb leg steaks, trimmed, about
    125g (4 ½oz) each
100g (4oz) baby carrots, halved
    lengthways
2 leeks, finely sliced
2 garlic cloves, crushed
salt and freshly ground black
    pepper
4 tablespoons mint sauce

Preheat the oven to 200°C/
Fan 180°C/Gas 6.

PREPARING AHEAD *Prepare completely a day ahead, wrapped in foil, ready to go in the oven.*

1 Heat a little oil in a non-stick frying pan and brown the lamb steaks for about 2 minutes on both sides until sealed and brown. Transfer to a plate.

2 Add the carrots and leeks to the unwashed pan and stir-fry over a high heat for about 5 minutes or until the carrots are starting to soften. Add the garlic and season with salt and pepper.

3 Prepare four pieces of foil about 20cm (8in) square, and fold in half to lie flat, like an open-sided envelope. Open the foil out again, and place each lamb steak on one-half of the foil. Spread 1 tablespoon of mint sauce over each lamb steak and top with the vegetable mixture. Fold over the other half of foil to make a parcel and seal the edges tightly together (rather like a Cornish pasty).

4 Transfer the parcels to a baking sheet and bake in the preheated oven for about 15-20 minutes until the lamb is cooked through.

5 To serve, carefully lift the lamb out of the parcels on to hot plates with the vegetables on top and pour over the juices from the parcel.

GOOD THINGS TO KNOW *You can vary the toppings for the lamb steaks. Brown the steaks as above, and bake in foil as above, simply with a different topping.*

For a Provençal topping, *add a little oil to the lamb pan, add 1 chopped onion, cover and simmer over low heat for about 5 minutes. Add 1 red pepper, seeded and thinly sliced, 1 sliced medium courgette, 1 crushed*

*garlic clove and 1 x 227g can chopped tomatoes.
Continue to simmer, covered, for about 5 minutes or
until the pepper and courgette are starting to soften.
Season and pile on top of the browned steak.*

For a hummus and red onion topping, *add a little oil to
the lamb pan, add 1 finely sliced red onion, cover and
simmer over a low heat for about 10 minutes. Remove
the lid, add 1 teaspoon brown sugar and cook
uncovered for a further 5 minutes until golden brown.
Spread 2 tablespoons hummus on top of each lamb
steak and top with the onion marmalade.*

AGA Slide on to the lowest set of runners in the roasting
oven for about 15 minutes.

Roast Fillet of Lamb with Buttered Leeks and Sherry Sauce

The true fillet of lamb is the eye of the loin – very expensive but very special. You buy them trimmed and boneless from your butcher or good supermarket.

SERVES 4-6

Preparation time 10 minutes
Cooking time 15 minutes

about 600g (1lb 6oz) lamb fillet,
    fully trimmed, boneless
1-2 tablespoons olive oil
salt and freshly ground black
    pepper
2 sprigs fresh rosemary
2-3 garlic cloves, cut in half
450g (1lb) leeks, trimmed (keep
    the trimmings)
a knob of butter

SAUCE

leek trimmings, roughly chopped
1 tablespoon olive oil
a knob of butter
1 level dessertspoon plain flour
300ml (½ pint) lamb or beef stock
2 tablespoons medium sherry
1 tablespoon redcurrant jelly
Worcestershire sauce to taste
a few drops of balsamic vinegar

Preheat the oven to 200°C/
Fan 180°C/Gas 6.

PREPARING AHEAD Brown the lamb and set aside on the rosemary and garlic, allow to cool, cover and leave in the fridge until ready to cook. To cook to serve, bring the lamb to room temperature and roast as above. The sauce can be made and strained ahead and reheated to serve. Cook the leeks just before serving.

1 Preheat a frying pan until very hot. Roll the lamb fillet in olive oil and pepper. Sear the lamb in the very hot pan for 1-1 ½ minutes on each side.

2 Lie the fillets on a bed of rosemary and garlic in a roasting tin. (This can all be done in advance to this stage, and allowed to become completely cold.)

3 Slide into the preheated oven for about 7-10 minutes, depending on the thickness of the lamb. Allow the lamb to rest for 5-10 minutes, and add any juices from the roasting tin to the finished sauce.

4 To make the sauce, fry the leek trimmings in the oil and butter over high heat for a few minutes, then blend in the flour. Gradually add the stock and sherry, bring to the boil, then add the redcurrant jelly. Stir, season with salt and pepper, and add the Worcestershire sauce and balsamic vinegar. Strain the sauce into a saucepan to serve.

5 Slice the leeks very thinly on the diagonal and fry in a little butter, stirring all the time. Season. Serve with the carved lamb and gravy.

GOOD THINGS TO KNOW If you have leeks in the garden, use them, but they will take a little longer to cook.

AGA Fry the fillets in a frying pan on the boiling plate. Roast on the second set of runners in the roasting oven for about 6-8 minutes. Rest for 5 minutes in the simmering oven before carving.

Butterflied Leg of Lamb with Garlic and Dijon Mustard Glaze

A fast roast, which can be ready in under an hour, and because it is boned, there are no carving problems! It is also wonderful when cooked on the barbecue.

SERVES 6-8

Preparation time 10 minutes
Cooking time 45 minutes

1 x 1.4kg (3lb) butterflied leg of lamb
2 garlic cloves, sliced
2 fresh rosemary sprigs, leaves removed
4 tablespoons Dijon mustard
2 tablespoons olive oil
2 tablespoons demerara sugar
salt and freshly ground black pepper

SAUCE

150ml (¼ pint) white wine
1 tablespoon redcurrant jelly
1 x 200ml carton full-fat crème fraîche

Preheat the oven to 200°C/ Fan 180°C/Gas 6.

PREPARING AHEAD

The lamb can be prepared and topped earlier on in the day, ready for roasting to serve.

1 Put the lamb cut-side down in a large roasting tin. Make about 15 holes using a sharp knife through the top fat into the flesh. Stuff each hole with the garlic slices and rosemary leaves.

2 Mix the mustard, oil and sugar together in a small bowl. Spread this mixture over the top of the lamb, and then season well.

3 Roast in the preheated oven for about 45 minutes (15 minutes per 450g/1lb).

4 Once cooked transfer to a plate, cover with foil and set aside to rest and keep warm for about 10-15 minutes.

5 Put the unwashed roasting tin over a high heat, and add the wine and redcurrant jelly. Deglaze, scraping the juices with a wooden spoon, and allow the wine to reduce by half.

6 Add the crème fraîche to the tin, along with any meat juices, bring to the boil and reduce again for a couple of minutes, taste and season.

7 Carve the lamb and serve with the hot sauce.

GOOD THINGS TO KNOW *Butterflied lamb is a boned leg of lamb, which is flattened out to give a rough butterfly shape. The joint cooks quickly and is easy to carve.*

AGA Slide on to the grid shelf on the floor of the roasting oven for about 40 minutes. Rest for 10 minutes or so in the simmering oven before carving.

Tuscan Lamb

No need to make a gravy with this recipe, as there is plenty of sauce with the beans. And if you have time, you can cook your own dried beans from scratch – soaking them overnight, and cooking until tender.

SERVES 6

Preparation time 10 minutes
Cooking time 1 hour 20 minutes

2 tablespoons olive oil
2 large onions, roughly chopped
2 garlic cloves, crushed
1 small boned shoulder of lamb, about 1.4kg (3lb) boned weight
salt and freshly ground black pepper
3 tablespoons sun-dried tomato paste
1 x 400g can chopped tomatoes
3 x 400g cans cannellini beans, drained and rinsed
100ml (4fl oz) white wine
1 tablespoon redcurrant jelly
1 tablespoon chopped fresh rosemary
2 tablespoons chopped fresh parsley

Preheat the oven to 180°C/ Fan 160°C/Gas 4.

PREPARING AHEAD *If you wanted, you could cook the beans separately with the tomatoes etc, up to a day ahead. Reheat when you roast the lamb.*

1 Measure the oil into a large roasting tin, and mix in the onions and garlic. Push to one end of the roasting tin.

2 Arrange the shoulder upside down at the other end of the roasting tin and season with salt and pepper. Roast in the preheated oven for about 40 minutes.

3 Turn the lamb over and spread with 2 tablespoons of the sun-dried tomato paste. Stir all the remaining ingredients – including the remaining paste, and omitting the parsley – into the onions. Push up to one end of the roasting tin again, and cover this end of the roasting tin with foil.

4 Continue to roast for a further 40 minutes until the lamb is crisp and brown and cooked to your taste.

5 Carve the lamb and serve with the beans and sauce, sprinkled with chopped parsley.

GOOD THINGS TO KNOW *This cooking time will mean the lamb is just pink in the middle. If you are worried about cooking times for meat, I would suggest buying a meat thermometer, they are very good and can put your mind at rest. If you want well-cooked lamb, cook it for a little longer.*

AGA Roast on the grid shelf on the floor of the roasting oven for about 1 hour 20 minutes. Keep an eye on the lamb for the last part of the cooking, and cover with foil if getting too brown.

Roasted Rack of Lamb with Cumberland Gravy

Rack of lamb is a roast for a special occasion. Use orange juice from a carton for the marinade, which becomes the sauce.

SERVES 4-6
Preparation time 10 minutes, plus marinating time
Cooking time 30 minutes

2 racks of lamb, French trimmed, chined
3 fresh rosemary sprigs

MARINADE

250ml (9floz) orange juice
1 tablespoon redcurrant jelly
2 tablespoons honey
3 tablespoons soy sauce
2 fat garlic cloves, crushed
2 teaspoons tomato purée

ROASTED VINE TOMATOES

12-18 small tomatoes left on the vine
olive oil
salt and freshly ground black pepper
2 garlic cloves, crushed
1 tablespoon balsamic vinegar

Preheat the oven to 220°C/
Fan 200°C/Gas 7.

PREPARING AHEAD *The lamb can be left to marinate for up to two days.*

1 Insert sprigs of rosemary between each cutlet bone.

2 Combine all the marinade ingredients. Take two large freezer bags and put one inside the other. Pour the marinade into the inner bag and add the lamb. Seal and leave to marinate for as long as possible, turning occasionally.

3 Drain the lamb, reserving the marinade. Put the lamb in a roasting tin, fat-side up, and roast in the preheated oven for about 20-25 minutes. Add the marinade halfway through the cooking time. Check the joint after about 15 minutes; if the skin is getting too brown, cover with foil. When done skim off any surplus fat from the juices in the tin, and check the seasoning.

4 Allow the lamb to rest for about 15 minutes covered with foil.

5 Meanwhile, for the tomatoes, roll the tomatoes in oil, salt, pepper and garlic in a small roasting tin (this can be done ahead). Slide into the preheated oven for about 5 minutes whilst resting the lamb. Spoon over the balsamic vinegar.

6 Carve the racks of lamb into chops and serve with the gravy and roasted vine tomatoes.

GOOD THINGS TO KNOW *The cooking time will vary according to the size of the racks of lamb. Marks & Spencer racks are small and beautifully trimmed, so are cooked in about 20 minutes. Sometimes racks from butchers and other supermarkets are larger, so take longer. Each rack has seven cutlets (chops). French trimmed means that all surplus fat is removed, the rib bones are cut short and the chine bone is removed which makes carving easy as you just cut straight between the bones. The joints take a very short time to cook.*

AGA Slide on to the second set of runners in the roasting oven for about 20 minutes.

Roast Fillet of Pork with Cranberry and Madeira Gravy

For a roast, this impressive dish is easy to do. It is a fast recipe as it can be made ahead and cooked to serve, and it carves easily. It is two pork fillets, flattened out, then filled with a mushroom stuffing and wrapped in bacon.

SERVES 6

Preparation time 15 minutes
Cooking time 1 hour

2 pork fillets of equal length, each about 450g (1lb) in weight, trimmed of all fat
10-12 long rashers of streaky bacon
salt and freshly ground black pepper

STUFFING

1 tablespoon sunflower oil
1 medium onion. finely chopped
225g (8oz) chestnut mushrooms, chopped
40g (1 ½oz) Parmesan, freshly grated
25g (1oz) fresh white breadcrumbs
3-4 tablespoons chopped fresh parsley
1 teaspoon chopped fresh thyme
1 egg yolk

CRANBERRY AND MADEIRA GRAVY

25g (1oz) butter
100g (4oz) chestnut mushrooms, sliced
300ml (½ pint) cranberry juice
75ml (2 ½fl oz) Madeira
1 rounded tablespoon plain flour
2 tablespoons balsamic vinegar

Preheat the oven to 220°C/
Fan 200°C/Gas 7.

1 First make the stuffing. Heat the oil in a frying pan, add the onion and fry for a few minutes over a low heat until tender. Add the chopped mushrooms to the onion, and cook over a high heat to drive off any liquid from the mushrooms. When the pan is completely dry, take off the heat and add all the remaining stuffing ingredients, seasoning with salt and pepper. Set aside to cool.

2 Split the pork fillets lengthways halfway through (but not entirely in half), open out and cover with clingfilm. Using a rolling pin, beat out to flatten. Stretch the bacon rashers with the back of a knife, and arrange overlapping on a chopping board.

3 Put one fillet on top of the bacon, season with black pepper, and spread with the stuffing. Cover with the other fillet, beaten side facing down. Roll up tightly, folding each piece of bacon over the roll. Lift into a roasting tin with the bacon join underneath.

4 Bake in the preheated oven for about an hour until the bacon is crisp and the pork is cooked.

5 While the pork is roasting, make the gravy. Melt the butter in a saucepan, add the sliced mushrooms, and cook for a few minutes. Gradually pour in the cranberry juice. In a small bowl blend the Madeira with the flour until smooth, then add to the sauce. Bring to the boil, stirring, then add the balsamic vinegar. Season with salt and pepper.

6 Allow the pork to rest for a minimum of 10 minutes. Add the roasting tin juices to the gravy if they are not too salty.

7 Carve the pork and serve with the gravy and some mashed potato.

PREPARING AHEAD *Prepare the fillets a day ahead, and roast to serve.*

GOOD THINGS TO KNOW *For a different stuffing in winter, replace the mushrooms in the stuffing with 225g (8oz) frozen thawed chestnuts, coarsely chopped. Fry in the pan before the onions with a little butter and oil.*

AGA Cook at the top of the roasting oven for about an hour until tender and brown.

Mango-glazed Gammon with Mango and Mint Salsa

Ham is always a top favourite, whether served hot or cold. If cooking a ham near Christmas time, the ham skin is excellent placed over the turkey breast for roasting to keep the breast moist. Gammon is a raw cured bacon leg cut, and it is called ham when it is cooked. This needs so little preparation, it is the fastest cut-and-come-again meat to do for a crowd.

SERVES ABOUT 12

Preparation time 10 minutes
Cooking time this depends on the size of the gammon (see below)

1 x 2.6 kg (6lb) gammon
1 x 1 litre carton orange and
    mango juice or tropical fruit juice
mango chutney to glaze
a few cloves

SALSA

about 4 tablespoons mango
    chutney
1 large mango, peeled and neatly
    chopped
1 small fresh red chilli, seeded and
    finely chopped
2.5cm (1in) piece fresh root ginger,
    peeled and grated
4 tablespoons chopped fresh mint
1 tablespoon white wine vinegar
finely grated rind and juice of 1
    lime

PREPARING AHEAD *You can cook and brown the gammon one or two days ahead, and then cool and chill it. Don't carve too soon, though, or the gammon will lose its pink colour*

1 Weigh the joint and calculate the cooking time. Allow 20 minutes per 450g (1lb) and 20 minutes over.

2 Put the joint in a saucepan just big enough to take it, and cover with the fruit juice and lid. (Add some water if not covered completely.) Bring to the boil over a high heat, turn the heat down and simmer very gently for the calculated time.

3 About 5 minutes before the end of the cooking time, preheat the grill.

4 Remove the gammon from the juice (reserve the juice). Leave to cool slightly. Cut off any string, and peel off the skin. Spread mango chutney thickly over the fatty surface. Score the fat to make a lattice pattern, and stud with a few cloves.

5 Cover the lean meat around the sides with foil and put the gammon in a grill pan lined with foil. Pour some of the reserved juice inside the foil and slide the gammon under the hot grill until golden brown and an even colour.

6 For the salsa, simply mix all the ingredients together and serve with the hot or cold gammon.

GOOD THINGS TO KNOW *Check with your butcher when you buy your gammon whether or not it needs to be soaked before cooking to remove the saltiness. Supermarket gammon usually does not need soaking as the cure is milder.*

AGA Put the gammon snugly in a large pan. Cover with fruit juice as above. Bring to the boil on the boiling plate, cover and transfer to the simmering oven to cook. It will take about 2-3 hours until it is tender. Brown towards the top of the roasting oven for about 15 minutes, turning round once.

Sausage, Leek and Potato Pie

You could make this with fresh leftover vegetables from Sunday lunch. Just cut them up – using, say, some carrots, parsnips, boiled potatoes and a few frozen peas. Add them to the cheese sauce with about 225g (8oz) cubed cooked ham. Arrange in a dish, sprinkle with grated cheese, and heat and brown in a hot oven for about 20 minutes. (You omit the sausages, of course!) The pie is very quick as the vegetables are boiled in one pan, adding them in succession, with the fastest-cooking ones last.

SERVES 4

Preparation time 10 minutes
Cooking time 10 minutes

250g (9oz) large potatoes, peeled
   and cut into 2.5cm (1in) pieces
salt and freshly ground black
   pepper
250g (9oz) carrots, peeled and cut
   into 2.5cm (1in) pieces
2 leeks, cut into thick rings
8 good pork sausages

CHEESE SAUCE

25g (1oz) butter
25g (1oz) plain flour
300ml (½ pint) milk
100g (4oz) mature Cheddar,
   grated
1 teaspoon Dijon mustard

Preheat the grill to its maximum.
You will need a shallow ovenproof
dish, capacity of about 1.7 litres
(3 pints).

PREPARING AHEAD *Cook all the vegetables ahead, and put them into the sauce.*

1 Boil the potatoes in salted water for about 5 minutes until beginning to soften, then add the carrots and leeks and boil for a further 5 minutes until tender. Drain.

2 Whilst the vegetables are cooking, arrange the sausages on the grill pan and cook under the hot grill until golden brown on one side. Remove and set aside.

3 To make the cheese sauce, melt the butter in a pan, add the flour and stir to form a roux. Gradually whisk in the milk, and bring to the boil, whisking all the time, to make a smooth sauce. Add half the cheese, the mustard and some salt and pepper.

4 Mix the vegetables and sauce together, and arrange in the ovenproof dish. Sprinkle the remaining cheese over the top, and arrange the sausages, browned-side down, over the surface of the dish, sitting in the vegetable mixture.

5 Return to the grill to brown, about 10 minutes. Keep an eye on it. Serve at once when piping hot.

GOOD THINGS TO KNOW *For vegetarians, forget the sausages and increase the cheese to 150g (5oz), or alternatively use vegetarian sausages. For a faster cheese sauce, heat the milk until piping hot then add to the butter and flour roux. Not only is it quicker, but it means the sauce is less likely to be lumpy using the hot milk – great when time is important.*

AGA Follow steps 1, 3 and 4 then brown sausages on one side in a frying pan. Top the vegetable dish with sausages (browned-side down) and slide on to the top set of runners in the roasting oven for about 30 minutes.

Fast Sauces

Gravy If you buy a jar or carton of gravy from the supermarket give it your own stamp. Taste first, then add a little Worcestershire sauce, a dash of lemon juice and, if need be, a spoonful of redcurrant jelly. A little red wine or dry sherry may well improve it too. Don't forget that, if there are any juices from the meat, you should tip them in as well.

White Sauce Use hot milk instead of cold, it works in more quickly. With fish or with cauliflower, a good dollop of French mustard goes well, and with beef some horseradish sauce.

Fresh Herb Sauce One which goes with fish can be simply made by processing a small bunch of leafy herbs e.g. parsley, dill and tarragon, with equal quantities of mayonnaise and crème fraîche. Add a dash of lemon juice and season with salt and pepper to taste. Serve cold. Very good with cold salmon or trout.

Posh Mushroom Sauce Great with steak, chops or fish. Reduce 4 tablespoons white wine to 2 tablespoons and add 200ml (7fl oz) double cream. Stir well, and reduce again to a sauce consistency, then add 100g (4oz) sliced chestnut button mushrooms, pepper and salt. Cook for a few more minutes. If serving with fish, add some chopped tarragon or dill. Serve hot.

Antipasto of Smoked Fish and Prawns

This is a great idea for when time is short, and you want a smart but simple lunch. Serve with good warm bread or rolls and butter.

SERVES 6

Preparation time 10 minutes

12 quail's eggs

1 x 275g jar marinated herrings in dill marinade, drained

1 x 200g packet smoked mackerel fillets

6 smoked salmon slices

6 cooked Madagascan prawns, shell on

1 x 50g bag mixed salad leaves

1 lemon, cut into 6 wedges

HORSERADISH AND DILL SAUCE

6 tablespoons crème fraîche

2 tablespoons creamed horseradish sauce

2 tablespoons snipped fresh dill

salt and freshly ground black pepper

1 Put the quail's eggs in a saucepan. Cover with cold water, bring up to the boil then simmer for 3 minutes. Drain, refresh in cold water and peel.

2 For the sauce, mix the crème fraîche, horseradish and dill together in a small bowl, and season well.

3 Put the quail's eggs, dill sauce and herrings into three small bowls, scallop shells or ramekins, and arrange in a triangle shape near the centre of a large round plate.

4 Skin the mackerel, then flake into large pieces and arrange next to the sauce.

5 Arrange the smoked salmon and prawns in the remaining gaps.

6 Place the mixed salad in a pile in the middle of the plate. Garnish with the lemon wedges.

GOOD THINGS TO KNOW *Quail's eggs are sometimes difficult to peel once boiled, like fresh hen eggs, as the white part of the egg clings to the shell. It is better to have them not too fresh. It also helps to peel them straightaway once they are cool enough to handle, so plunge into cold water after the 3 minutes' boiling and get peeling!*

Spiced Smoked Haddock and Parsley Fishcakes

For speed the fishcakes are coated in crushed cheese biscuits – cream crackers. If you have white breadcrumbs in the freezer, use them if preferred.

SERVES 4-6, MAKES 8 CAKES
Preparation time 20 minutes
Cooking time 10 minutes

450g (1lb) old potatoes, peeled
  and cut into 5cm (2in) cubes
2 eggs
salt and freshly ground black
  pepper
450g (1lb) smoked haddock fillet,
  skinned and cut into 5cm (2in)
  cubes
3 tablespoons milk
1 ½ teaspoons medium curry
  powder
3 tablespoons mango chutney
4 tablespoons chopped fresh
  parsley
juice of ½ lemon
6 cream crackers, finely crushed
2 tablespoons sunflower oil

PREPARING AHEAD *Make a day ahead and chill in the fridge until you need them.*

1 Put the potatoes and eggs into two separate saucepans. Cover with water, add salt to the potatoes, and boil for 10 minutes or until the potatoes are tender. Drain the potatoes and mash. Drain the eggs after 10 minutes and plunge into cold water; when cold, peel and roughly chop.

2 Meanwhile put the fish and milk into a small deep saucepan, cover and bring to the boil. Simmer gently for about 2 minutes until the fish is just cooked. Spoon the haddock into a large mixing bowl (check for any bones). Add a little of the hot fishy liquid to the mashed potatoes and beat until smooth.

3 Add the curry powder, mango chutney, parsley and lemon juice to the fish in the bowl, along with the chopped eggs. Season well with pepper and a little salt, and mix in the mash. Be careful to keep the fish fairly chunky. If the mixture is a bit soft to shape, chill until easier to handle.

4 Divide the mixture into eight, then shape, using your hands, into eight round cakes. Coat the cakes in the crushed crackers.

5 Heat a little oil in a frying pan and when hot, fry the cakes for about 4-5 minutes on each side or until golden brown and piping hot.

6 Serve at once with a quick fresh tarragon sauce (see page 58). If you are not fond of tarragon use the same amount of fresh dill instead.

GOOD THINGS TO KNOW *You can vary the fishcakes.*

For Thai fishcakes, *use the same amount of fish and potatoes as above. Change the smoked haddock to fresh haddock. Omit the curry powder, lemon and* *chutney, and add 1 teaspoon of Thai curry paste, 2 tablespoons sweet chilli sauce and the juice of ½ lime.*

For grainy mustard fishcakes, *use the same amount of fish and potatoes as above. Omit the curry powder, lemon and chutney, and replace with 3 sliced spring onions, 2 tablespoons grainy mustard and 50g (2oz) strong Cheddar, grated.*

For salmon and prawn fishcakes, cook the potatoes as above. Replace the haddock with 350g (12oz) fresh salmon fillet, skinned, and 100g (4oz) cooked shelled prawns, roughly chopped. Omit the curry powder and chutney, and replace with 2 tablespoons mayonnaise and 2 tablespoons chopped fresh parsley. Cook salmon as above and stir in the prawns with the other ingredients.

Twice-baked Cheese and Prawn Terrine

A classic roulade base, layered rather than rolled. It reheats brilliantly and is an ideal dish for a light lunch or supper.

SERVES 6

Preparation time 20 minutes
Cooking time 15 minutes

1 x 150g packet Boursin cheese
5 eggs, separated
150g (5oz) mature Cheddar, grated
4-5 tablespoons chopped fresh parsley
150g (5oz) shelled cooked prawns
salt and freshly ground black pepper
a little Parmesan cheese, grated

BECHAMEL SAUCE

45g (1 ½oz) butter
45g (1 ½oz) plain flour
450ml (¾ pint) hot milk
½ teaspoon Dijon mustard
a good dash of Tabasco sauce

Preheat the oven to 220°C/ Fan 200°C/Gas 7. Line a 23 x 33cm (9 x 13in) Swiss roll tin with non-stick paper.

PREPARING AHEAD

The assembled terrine can be wrapped in clingfilm and left in the fridge for up to 24 hours before the final reheating. If baked from cold, it will take a little longer.

1 For the béchamel sauce, melt the butter in a large saucepan, add the flour and stir over a high heat. Slowly add the hot milk, whisking until thick and smooth. Bring to the boil, and season with salt, pepper, mustard and a dash of Tabasco.

2 Reserve 150ml (¼ pint) of the sauce for the filling. Mix the Boursin cheese into this reserved sauce quantity (which is easier to do when the sauce is hot).

3 Allow the remainder of the sauce to cool slightly whilst whisking the egg whites with an electric hand whisk until stiff. Fold 2 tablespoons of egg white into the cooled sauce, then stir in the egg yolks, grated Cheddar and parsley. Fold in the rest of the whisked egg whites.

4 Pour this soufflé mixture into the prepared tin and level the top. Cook in the preheated oven for about 10-15 minutes or until golden brown and set in the middle. Allow to cool slightly before turning out on to a clean sheet of non-stick paper. Trim the edges and cut lengthways into three equal strips about 7cm (2 ¾in) wide.

5 Put one strip of the terrine on to a long buttered ovenproof plate or flat dish, and spread with half the Boursin mixture. Lay half the prawns over the top, and season with salt and pepper. Spread a small amount of Boursin mixture on the underneath side of the next strip (to ensure it sticks to the prawns) and sit on top. Repeat with the next layer and finish with the last strip of terrine. Sprinkle the top with Parmesan.

6 To cook for the second time, cook at the same temperature for about 12-15 minutes until piping hot.

7 Serve at once with a dressed rocket salad.

GOOD THINGS TO KNOW *You can make your own version of herb cheese if you have fresh herbs in* *the garden in the summer. Mix 150g (5oz) cream cheese with 2 crushed garlic cloves, some black pepper, a dash of salt and a handful of chopped fresh leafy herbs.*

AGA Bake at first on the grid shelf on the floor of the roasting oven for about 10 minutes until golden brown and set in the middle. If getting brown, slide the cold sheet on to the second set of runners. To cook for the second time, slide the buttered ovenproof dish on to the second set of runners of the roasting oven for about 12 minutes.

Triple Fish and Broccoli Bake

This dish is perfect for feeding the family or friends for supper. It can be made ahead of time, and simply popped into the hot oven to serve.

SERVES 4-6

Preparation time 15 minutes
Cooking time 20-25 minutes

225g (8oz) broccoli
salt and freshly ground black
    pepper
1 tablespoon cornflour
1 x 400ml carton half-fat crème
    fraîche
75g (3oz) Parmesan, grated
2 teaspoons Dijon mustard
300g (10oz) salmon fillet, skinned
    and sliced into 5cm (2in) cubes
300g (10oz) cod fillet, skinned and
    sliced into 5cm (2in) cubes
75g (3oz) shelled prawns
50g (2oz) fresh breadcrumbs

Preheat the oven to 220°C/
Fan 200°C/Gas 7. You will need
an ovenproof dish, with a capacity
of about 1.7 litres (3 pints).

PREPARING AHEAD *Prepare completely 24 hours in advance, and keep in the fridge. The baking from cold will take slightly longer.*

1 Trim the broccoli into small florets. Use the stalks too if you like (see below). Bring a pan of salted water up to a rolling boil. Add the broccoli florets and boil for about 3-4 minutes, then drain and refresh in cold water until cold. Dry well, and set aside.

2 Mix the cornflour with 3 tablespoons of the crème fraîche in a bowl, then add the rest of the crème fraîche, half the cheese and all the mustard. Fold in the salmon, cod, prawns and broccoli, and season with salt and pepper. Spoon into the ovenproof dish.

3 Sprinkle the top of the dish with breadcrumbs and the remaining cheese. Bake in the centre of the preheated oven for about 20-25 minutes until golden brown on top, bubbling around the edges and the fish is cooked.

GOOD THINGS TO KNOW *Crème fraîche can be bought as full fat or half fat. When heating for a sauce for pasta or any hot dish, it is important to use full fat as the half-fat version contains more water and goes very thin and runny. If using full-fat crème fraîche in hot dishes it is reasonably thick once reduced a little. With half-fat crème fraîche you will need to add a stabiliser such as cornflour as in this recipe, otherwise it will be too runny. The half-fat version is perfect for cold dishes, or in a sauce to go with fish, mixed with fresh herbs.*

AND ANOTHER THING *Broccoli stalks can be eaten as well as the florets. Take the whole stalk, trim off the end, then peel off the tough outer skin. Cut the stalk into short pencil strips. They will cook just as quickly as the florets, as long as you have taken off the outer skin beforehand.*

AGA Slide the dish on to the grid shelf on the floor of the roasting oven for about 25 minutes.

Gleneagles Salmon

This recipe is perfect for a cold buffet or cooking for numbers, and makes an ideal replacement for the poached salmon that seems to appear at every charity function! It is very light with no mayonnaise or cream, and looks very attractive with its herb dressing.

SERVES 6

Preparation time 20 minutes
Cooking time 20 minutes, plus marinating time

6 x 150g (5oz) middle-cut salmon
   fillets, skinned
salt and freshly ground black
   pepper
about 12 asparagus tips
1 very small fennel bulb, halved,
   core removed, thinly sliced
   lengthways into long strips
4 spring onions, sliced thinly on the
   diagonal
6 thin smoked salmon slices

DRESSING

150ml (¼ pint) good olive oil
4 tablespoons lemon juice
2 tablespoons honey
2 teaspoons Dijon mustard
2 tablespoons each of chopped
   fresh parsley, chives and basil

Preheat the oven to 180°C/
Fan 160°C/Gas 4.

PREPARING AHEAD *Cook the salmon, and marinate a day ahead in half the dressing without the herbs (if you add the herbs they will lose their colour). The vegetables for the bundle can be cooked and prepared and kept in the fridge overnight. Assemble all on the day and add the herbs to the dressing.*

1. Line a small roasting tin with foil, leaving a good overhang. Season the foil and lie the salmon fillets on top. Season the top of the salmon, and fold the overhang of foil over the fish, pressing tightly to seal the edges.

2. Bake in the preheated oven for about 10-15 minutes until just cooked. Carefully lift out on to a shallow oblong dish, and remove the foil.

3. Mix all the dressing ingredients together and spoon all but 3 tablespoons of the dressing over the warm salmon fillets. Leave to marinate until cool, or about 2 hours.

4. Blanch the asparagus in boiling water for about 4 minutes, drain and refresh in cold water. Dry the asparagus well and mix with the fennel and spring onion, then toss in the remaining dressing and leave to marinate.

5. Lay the slices of smoked salmon on a board, divide the vegetables between each, then roll up to give six sausage shapes.

6. Lift the salmon fillets on to a plate and top each with a smoked salmon bundle. Pinch the smoked salmon in the centre of each bundle. Serve cold with the dressing.

GOOD THINGS TO KNOW *Buy long thin slices of smoked salmon for this recipe – often called cocktail slices. These will be much easier to wrap round the vegetables.*

AGA Cook the foil-covered salmon on the grid shelf on the floor of the roasting oven for about 10 minutes until just cooked.

Fast Lane Salmon

A very speedy and stylish fish recipe, which is ideal for large numbers as no last-minute attention is needed. When heating the sauce in the pan, bubble until a good sauce consistency, then add the cucumber and spring onion just before serving, otherwise the sauce will be too runny.

SERVES 4

Preparation time 10 minutes
Cooking time 12-15 minutes

1 x 375g packet ready-rolled puff pastry
4 x 150g (5oz) centre-cut salmon fillets, skinned
salt and freshly ground black pepper
1 x 200ml carton full-fat crème fraîche
50g (2oz) Parmesan, grated
½ cucumber, peeled, seeded and chopped to the size of a pine nut
2-3 spring onions, finely chopped
2 tablespoons chopped fresh parsley
1 egg, beaten

Preheat the oven to 200°C/ Fan 180°C/Gas 6.

PREPARING AHEAD *The fish can be all prepared and wrapped in pastry, covered in clingfilm and kept in the fridge for up to 24 hours ahead.*

1 Roll out half the pastry very thinly and cut into four oblong shapes, each about 7.5 x 15cm (3 x 6in).

2 Season the salmon fillets with salt and pepper.

3 Mix the crème fraîche with half the Parmesan and some salt and pepper. Spread a teaspoon of crème fraîche on to the centre of each fillet, and sprinkle with a tiny amount of the cucumber, spring onion and chopped parsley.

4 Wrap a strip of puff pastry around each fillet, over the crème fraîche mixture, ensuring the join is underneath. Arrange on a baking sheet. Lightly score the pastry in a lattice pattern and brush with a little beaten egg. Sprinkle with the remaining Parmesan.

5 Bake the parcels in the preheated oven for about 12-15 minutes until the pastry is crisp and the salmon is cooked right through.

6 To make the sauce, heat the remaining crème fraîche in a small pan until just hot. Just before serving add the remaining cucumber, spring onion and parsley, and season with salt and pepper. Serve hot with the hot salmon.

GOOD THINGS TO KNOW *If time is short, omit the cucumber and spring onion on top of the fish – just add it all to the sauce.*

AGA Cook the salmon parcels on the floor of the roasting oven for about 8 minutes, then turn the baking sheet round and transfer to the top of the roasting oven

Salmon en Croute Fast and Special

This pastry-wrapped salmon is wonderful for a party, and looks very good. If using peppers from a jar instead of freshly roasted, drain well and cut into thick strips.

SERVES 12

Preparation time 15 minutes
Cooking time 30-40 minutes

4 red peppers or 1 x 280g jar
    roasted mixed peppers
1 x 375g packet ready-rolled puff
    pastry
2 x 700g (1 ½lb) pieces fillet of
    salmon, skinned
salt and freshly ground black
    pepper
3 tablespoons chopped fresh basil
1 egg, beaten

SAUCE

300ml (½ pint) double cream
juice of ½ lemon
2 tablespoons green pesto
2 tablespoons chopped fresh basil

Preheat the oven to 220°C/ Fan
200°C /Gas 7, and preheat a
baking sheet to get very hot.

PREPARING AHEAD *The uncooked finished salmon may be left in the fridge for up to 24 hours.*

1 If using fresh peppers, cut in half, remove the seeds and place cut-side down on to a baking sheet. Slide into the preheated oven for about 30 minutes until charred and soft. Transfer to an oiled bowl, cover tightly with clingfilm (or put in a sealed poly bag), and leave until cool enough to handle. Remove the skin from the peppers and cut the flesh into thick strips. If using a jar, drain and cut the peppers into thick strips.

2 Roll the pastry large enough to wrap the salmon, about 33 x 44cm (13 x 17 ½in).

3 Place one fillet of salmon on to the centre of the pastry, season with salt and pepper, and arrange the peppers and basil on top. Season the second side of salmon, and place on top of the other one so it mirrors the underneath one.

4 Cut straight horizontal slits about 2.5 cm (1in) wide, from the pastry stretching out on either side of the salmon, cutting from the salmon outwards to the edge of the pastry. Lift the cut strips of pastry across the fish to form a plait. Start from the broadest end of the fish, alternating between each side. Brush with egg glaze.

5 Carefully transfer to the hot baking sheet in the preheated oven, and bake for about 30-40 minutes until golden brown. Rest for 10 minutes before slicing.

6 To make the sauce, heat the cream, add lemon juice, pesto and season. Add the basil just before serving.

7 Serve the salmon hot in slices with the hot sauce.

GOOD THINGS TO KNOW *If time is short, simply wrap the salmon in the pastry as you would do for beef Wellington.*

AGA Cook on grid shelf on floor of the roasting oven for about 20 minutes; remove the grid shelf and cook directly on the floor for a further 20 minutes until golden brown.

Grilled Rainbow Trout with Parsley and Caper Butter Sauce

All very simple, but with interesting flavours. The fish go well with new potatoes and purple-sprouting broccoli.

SERVES 4

Preparation time 5 minutes
Cooking time 16 minutes

4 rainbow trout, about 225g (8oz) each, gutted and cleaned
about 75g (3oz) butter, softened
salt and freshly ground black pepper
1 small lemon
2 teaspoons capers, drained and rinsed
2 tablespoons chopped fresh parsley

Preheat the grill to medium.

PREPARING AHEAD *You can put the fish ready to go in the grill pan a couple of hours in advance.*

1 Remove the rack from the grill pan, and line the pan with foil. Spread with half the butter and season the foil well with salt and pepper. Arrange the fish on the foil, spread with the remaining butter and season again with salt and pepper.

2 Grill the fish under medium heat for about 8 minutes on each side until brown and cooked through. Lift the fish on to warm plates and rest and keep hot. Pour the butter into a small bowl.

3 Cut the lemon in half, squeeze the juice from half and cut the remaining half into 4 wedges.

4 Add the lemon juice, capers and parsley to the butter in the bowl, season and stir. Pour the butter sauce over the fish to serve, and garnish with lemon wedges.

GOOD THINGS TO KNOW *Trout is less expensive than most fresh fish and is best, I think served whole, without stuffing as the stuffing is inclined to get mixed up with the bones. The bones are generally easy to free from the flesh.*

AND ANOTHER THING *Take care not to overcook the trout – 8 minutes on each side is fine – but if the grill is inefficient it may take longer. To test when done, check that the flesh turns opaque near the bones.*

AGA Cook in a buttered dish at the very top of the roasting oven for about 15-20 minutes.

Spiced Monkfish

Monkfish is expensive, but it is perfect for a special meal – just serve with a dressed green salad. You could use the same onion and rice filling to stuff small curled-round fillets of fish such as haddock or whiting.

SERVES 4
Preparation time 20 minutes
Cooking time 15 minutes

4 x 150g (5oz) monkfish tail fillets
butter
salt and freshly ground black
   pepper

FILLING

1 onion, roughly chopped
75g (3oz) long-grain rice
75g (3oz) butter
1 tablespoon medium curry
   powder
2 tablespoons lemon juice
1 tablespoon chopped fresh
   parsley
2 eggs, hard-boiled and roughly
   chopped

Preheat the oven to 200°C/
Fan 180°C/Gas 6, and butter and
season a roasting tin.

PREPARING AHEAD *Earlier in the day, you can stuff the fish. Keep in the fridge, covered.*

1 Put the onion and rice into a saucepan of boiling salted water and boil for about 10 minutes or until the rice is cooked and the onion is tender. Drain.

2 Melt the butter in the pan, add the rice and onion, and sprinkle in the curry powder. Fry over high heat for a minute or so. Stir in the lemon juice, parsley and chopped egg, and mix well. Check the seasoning, adding salt and pepper if needed.

3 Make a pocket in each monkfish fillet using a sharp knife, cutting top to bottom halfway through the fillet. Divide the rice mixture between the fillets, pushing it into the pocket.

4 Transfer the fillets to the prepared roasting tin, and season the top of the fish. Bake in the preheated oven for about 15 minutes or until the fish is cooked through and the filling is slightly brown on top.

GOOD THINGS TO KNOW *Par-boiled rice like Uncle Ben's is sometimes called easy-cook rice – it is a creamy colour and long-grained, and very good for savoury rice dishes.*

AGA Slide the roasting tin on to the second set of runners in the roasting oven for about 15 minutes until the fish is just cooked and the filling is brown on top.

Double Haddock and Dill Mornay

Everything here is cooked in one dish, which saves on washing up. This makes a real change from fish pie, as the potatoes are mixed in rather than served as a mash on top.

SERVES 6

Preparation time 20 minutes
Cooking time 30 minutes

500g (1lb 2oz) large potatoes, peeled and cut into 2cm (¾ in) cubes
salt and freshly ground black pepper
6 eggs
150ml (¼ pint) white wine
225g (8oz) button mushrooms
70g (2 ½oz) butter
50g (2oz) plain flour
900ml (1 ½ pints) milk
500g (1lb 2oz) undyed smoked haddock, cut into 2.5cm (1in) pieces
500g (1lb 2oz) fresh haddock, cut into 2.5cm (1in) pieces
a bunch of fresh dill, chopped
75g (3oz) mature Cheddar, grated
50g (2oz) fresh white breadcrumbs

Preheat the oven to 180°C/ Fan 160°C/Gas 4. You will need a buttered, shallow ovenproof dish, about 20 x 30cm (8 x 12in).

PREPARING AHEAD *Complete to step 6, cool and keep in the fridge for up to 12 hours. Bring back to room temperature and then cook as above. Or cook straight from the fridge but for a little longer.*

1 Boil the potatoes in boiling salted water for about 10 minutes until just tender, then drain and set aside.

2 Boil the eggs in boiling water for 10 minutes, drain and cool under cold water. Peel and cut into quarters.

3 Put the wine and mushrooms into a pan and boil for about 4 minutes until the wine has reduced by half. Using a slotted spoon, transfer the mushrooms to a plate and reserve the wine to add to the sauce.

4 To make the sauce, melt the butter in a saucepan, then off the heat add the flour. Return to the heat and gradually add the milk, whisking until thick and bubbling. Whisk in the reserved wine over a high heat until smooth. Season with salt and pepper.

5 Add the fish pieces and potatoes to the hot sauce and bring to the boil again. Add the cooked mushrooms and fresh dill.

6 Pour into a buttered shallow ovenproof dish, and push the egg quarters into the sauce. Sprinkle with cheese and breadcrumbs.

7 Bake in the preheated oven for about 30 minutes until bubbling and golden on top.

GOOD THINGS TO KNOW *If you have leftover boiled potatoes, this would be a very good way of using them up.*

AGA Slide the dish on to the top set of runners in the roasting oven for about 25 minutes.

Crusted Haddock Peperonata

This is the perfect recipe to prepare ahead as it is all cooked in one dish and popped in the oven. Peperonata is an Italian mixture of red peppers, tomatoes, onions and garlic cooked in olive oil. For this recipe I have added fennel too. It is usually served hot with fish or meats or cold as an antipasto.

SERVES 6
Preparation time 10 minutes
Cooking time 20 minutes

6 x 150g (5oz) fresh haddock fillets, skinned
salt and freshly ground black pepper
6 dessertspoons tartare sauce from a jar
about 50g (2oz) coarse breadcrumbs (leftover ciabatta bread makes good breadcrumbs)
a little paprika pepper
3 tablespoons chopped fresh parsley

PEPERONATA BASE
1–2 tablespoons olive oil
1 very large onion, roughly chopped
2 Romano red peppers, halved lengthways and thickly sliced
1 large fennel bulb, roughly chopped
2 garlic cloves, crushed
1 x 200g can chopped tomatoes
½ teaspoon caster sugar
2 tablespoons capers, drained and rinsed

Preheat the oven to 200°C/ Fan 180°C/Gas 6.

PREPARING AHEAD *Once prepared, the dish can be kept in the fridge for up to 12 hours, and then cooked for a little longer than given in the recipe.*

1 For the peperonata base, heat the oil in a large non-stick frying pan. Add the onion and fry over a high heat for a few minutes. Add the peppers, fennel, garlic and tomatoes to the onion, stir well and bring to the boil. Season with salt, pepper and sugar, and fry to drive off any water for about 10 minutes, stirring, until the onions and fennel start to soften. Stir in the capers and spoon on to a shallow, fairly flat, ovenproof dish.

2 Season the fish on both sides and arrange on top of the vegetables. Spread about 1 dessertspoon of tartare sauce on each fillet, and sprinkle with the coarse breadcrumbs seasoned with salt, pepper and paprika.

3 Put the dish in the preheated oven and bake for about 20 minutes until the fish is cooked and piping hot.

4 Sprinkle with chopped parsley and serve.

GOOD THINGS TO KNOW *It is important to drive off any liquid which comes out of the vegetables before spooning into the dish – otherwise the sauce will be very wet and runny.*

AGA Slide an ovenproof dish on to the grid shelf on the floor of the roasting oven for about 20 minutes until the fish is just cooked.

Dover Sole with Warm Tomato and Basil Salsa

Dover soles are the kings of the sea. I always cook them on the bone because the flavour is best this way. They are best cooked at the last moment.

SERVES 2
Preparation time 5 minutes
Cooking time 8-10 minutes

50g (2oz) butter, softened
2 Dover soles, skinned on both
   sides, head on
salt and freshly ground black
   pepper

TOMATO AND BASIL SALSA
150g (5oz) baby plum tomatoes,
   halved
1 small avocado, peeled and
   chopped into 2.5cm (1in) cubes
1 tablespoon capers, drained
2 teaspoons balsamic vinegar
1 ½ tablespoons olive oil
½ teaspoon caster sugar
2 tablespoons fresh basil leaves,
   roughly torn

Preheat the grill to a high heat,
and line the grill rack in the grill tray
with foil.

1 Spread the butter over both sides of the fish and season well with salt and pepper. Arrange on the foil on the grill rack.

2 Grill at the highest position under the hot grill for about 4-5 minutes on each side or until the fish is just cooked through and golden brown.

3 To make the salsa, measure all the ingredients, except the basil, into a small saucepan and gently warm through over a low heat for about 3 minutes.

4 Serve the salsa warm with the fish, adding the fresh basil to the salsa at the end.

GOOD THINGS TO KNOW *If you have to keep fish hot because you are not serving it straightaway, slightly undercook it then the fish will finish cooking whilst it is keeping hot in a warm oven.*

AGA Preheat a roasting tin on the floor of the roasting oven for about 5 minutes. Add the buttered sole to the tin and return to the top of the roasting oven for about 4 minutes on each side until cooked through and golden brown. Alternatively it can be cooked in a frying pan or ridged grill pan on the boiling plate.

Mediterranean Seafood Paella

Surprisingly simple to make, as once the ingredients are collected it will be on the table within the hour. Buy fresh mixed seafood from the fish counter or in bags in the frozen section if you are able to.

SERVES 4-6
Preparation time 15 minutes
Cooking time 30 minutes

2 tablespoons olive oil
100g (4oz) chorizo sausage, peeled and chopped into small cubes
2 chicken breasts, boneless and skinless, cut into 2.5cm (1in) cubes
1 onion, finely sliced
1 red pepper, seeded and diced
2 garlic cloves, crushed
350g (12oz) paella rice
150ml (¼ pint) white wine
1 x 4g packet saffron, mixed with 3 tablespoons hot water
1 litre (1¾pints) chicken stock
salt and freshly ground black pepper
100g (4oz) raw tiger prawns, without shell
100g (4oz) raw squid rings
12 large mussels, washed
6 large king prawns, in shells, head on
juice of 1 lemon
4 tablespoons chopped fresh parsley

PREPARING AHEAD *Do all the vegetable preparation in advance.*

1 Heat 1 tablespoon of the oil in a deep non-stick frying pan. Add the chorizo and brown over a high heat for about 3-4 minutes. Add the chicken and continue to brown all over. Transfer to a plate.

2 Add the remaining oil to the pan, with the onion, pepper and garlic, and stir over a high heat for about 3 minutes, until the onion is beginning to soften. Add the rice, wine, saffron and stock, and bring to the boil. Cover with a lid and simmer, stirring from time to time, for about 10-12 minutes, or until the rice is nearly cooked. Season with salt and pepper.

3 Add the browned chorizo and chicken, and cook uncovered over a high heat for about 4-5 minutes. Add the seafood and lemon juice, and cook for a further 2 minutes or until the seafood is cooked through.

4 Season, sprinkle with parsley and serve hot.

GOOD THINGS TO KNOW *Paella rice can be bought from good supermarkets. It is a shorter grain rice and has a slightly creamier texture, like risotto rice. If you cannot buy paella rice, just use long-grain rice.*

AND ANOTHER THING *You can also vary the ingredients if you like. Add clams and fresh fish like cod and omit the chicken for just a fish paella. For a meat paella, omit the fish and seafood, and add pre-cooked bacon and chicken drumsticks.*

Scallop, Parma Ham and Mango Kebabs

King scallops with the roe are expensive, but very special. This recipe would also be very good on a hot barbecue. You will need eight skewers.

SERVES 4, 2 SKEWERS EACH
Preparation time 10 minutes
Cooking time about 3 minutes!

6 slices Parma ham
24 king scallops
1 large mango
a little sunflower oil

PREPARING AHEAD *Make the skewers up earlier in the day, and keep in the fridge, covered.*

1 Slice each slice of Parma ham into four lengthways so you have 24 pieces of ham. Wrap each scallop in Parma ham so you have 24 parcels.

2 Peel the mango and remove the flesh either side of the centre stone. Cut the flesh into 24 large chunks.

3 Thread a scallop parcel on to each skewer, then a piece of mango, then repeat so you have 3 scallops and 3 pieces of mango on each skewer. Brush with a little oil.

4 Heat a large grill pan or non-stick frying pan until very hot. Fry the kebabs for about 1 minute on each side until golden brown, the scallops are cooked through and the ham is crisp. Rest for a few minutes before serving.

GOOD THINGS TO KNOW *A mango has a flat stone in the centre so cut either side of the stone to remove the flesh. It is not like an avocado, you cannot cut round the stone!*

CHAPTER 4
ITALIAN COLLECTION

The majority of the recipes in this chapter are, naturally enough, for pasta, which must be the prime 'Italian collection'. And pasta – which has become such a favourite with all of us – is perhaps the ultimate 'fast' food. Nothing could be simpler and quicker when you come home from work, hungry and tired, than to pop some pasta into boiling water to cook, and to heat up an already prepared sauce. Topped with some freshly grated Parmesan (though not on fish pasta, traditionally), you have a virtually instant and delicious supper.

There are a number of new and interesting pasta combinations here, none of which takes much time to prepare and cook, and all of which taste delicious. Most are just a matter of assembly, and Lucy, Lucinda and I have had some wonderful lunches while testing them! There are also some pasta dishes here which normally take longer to cook, like spaghetti bolognaise and lasagne. With the former, I have devised a way of speeding up the sauce (see page 127), and lasagne, to me, is the ultimate dish that can be prepared ahead – it can even be frozen.

I use dried pasta, which is what the Italians do. I'm very fond of fresh pasta, and I use it as a vegetable, but I wouldn't dream of making my own pasta at home, as you can buy such good quality. I would always make the sauce though, and I have added five new fast pasta sauces which can be prepared at the time or prepared ahead, and simply heated through with the pasta. One of the most essential things to remember when cooking pasta on its own, is to salt the water generously. You cannot season afterwards. Use a tablespoon of salt to a large pot of water. Gino de Campo, the lovely Italian chef with whom I sometimes appear on BBC's *Saturday Kitchen*, always emphasises this point, and it really is very important.

Two other recipes in this chapter use the risotto rice so characteristic of northern Italian cooking, and both are speedy to prepare. A third recipe is for a southern Italian pizza, but instead of making a pizza base, I have given a recipe for using some of those wonderful ready-to-bake ciabatta breads we can find so easily nowadays. Much simpler, quick to prepare, and really good to eat!

Warm Smoked Salmon Pappardelle

A really quick and smart main course, which is perfect for a kitchen supper or informal lunch. If you have any difficulty in buying pappardelle, use tagliatelle instead. And if asparagus is expensive, use small broccoli florets instead, but take care not to overcook them.

SERVES 4
Preparation time 5 minutes, plus marinating
Cooking time 15 minutes

225g (8oz) smoked salmon slices
225g (8oz) full-fat crème fraîche
2 tablespoons chopped fresh dill
2 tablespoons chopped fresh basil
   or chives
salt and freshly ground black
   pepper
225g (8oz) fresh asparagus tips,
   weight after trimming
300g (10oz) pappardelle pasta
juice of ½ lemon

PREPARING AHEAD *Up to 6 hours ahead, cook the pasta and asparagus. Once cooked, rinse in running cold water and drain. Marinate the salmon. To serve, heat a large pan of water and bring to the boil. Blanch the cooked pasta and asparagus for about 30 seconds until hot, then drain. Add the marinated salmon to the pan, heat for a minute, then add the pasta and serve.*

1 Cut the salmon into small bite-sized pieces. Mix the crème fraîche with the salmon and herbs. Season with black pepper and leave to marinate for about 30 minutes if time allows.

2 Cut about 2.5cm (1in) from the end of the asparagus tips and put the stalks and tips to one side in separate piles.

3 Cook the pappardelle in boiling salted water according to packet instructions. Add the asparagus stalks 6 minutes before the end of cooking and the tips 2 minutes before the end of cooking. Drain well.

4 Return to the hot pasta pan and to the heat, and quickly add the salmon and crème fraîche mixture. Mix well for a minute or so until the creamy mixture is piping hot.

5 Serve at once with a dressed green salad.

GOOD THINGS TO KNOW *Basil is a Mediterranean herb, so keep the cut herb out of the fridge, as it goes limp and black. If you have a plant in a pot, a windowsill in the sunlight is ideal.*

Ciabatta Pizza with Artichokes and Spinach (V)

Using ciabatta bread saves making a pizza dough, and it tastes good too.

SERVES 4
Preparation time 10 minutes
Cooking time 15 minutes

1 x 227g can chopped tomatoes
2 tablespoons sun-dried tomato
    paste
1 tablespoon olive oil
1 garlic clove, crushed
1 x 225g packet baby spinach,
    roughly chopped
salt and freshly ground black
    pepper
1 ready-to-bake ciabatta loaf,
    sliced in half lengthways
1 x 280g jar artichokes in oil,
    drained and roughly chopped
150g (5oz) Taleggio cheese, thinly
    sliced

Preheat the oven to 200°C/
Fan 180°C/Gas 6.

1 Mix the tomatoes with the sun-dried tomato paste in a small bowl.

2 Heat the oil in a large non-stick frying pan. Add the garlic and fry for a minute then add the spinach and stir-fry over a high heat until wilted. Season with salt and pepper.

3 Arrange the slices of bread on non-stick paper on a baking sheet. Spread the tomato mixture over the ciabatta slices, then top with the spinach and artichokes. Arrange the cheese over the topping.

4 Bake in the middle of the preheated oven for about 15 minutes or until golden brown on top and crispy underneath.

5 Cut each ciabatta slice in half, and serve hot with a dressed green salad.

GOOD THINGS TO KNOW *Taleggio is a rich soft cows' milk cheese from northern Italy. You could use leftover Camembert instead.*

AGA Bake on the floor of the roasting oven for about 10-15 minutes.

Minted Lamb Meatballs with Spaghetti

Good supermarkets sell minced lamb, usually minced shoulder. These meatballs do not need frying first, so they make for a quick and healthy supper dish. You could serve them with mashed potatoes too.

SERVES 6
Preparation time 15 minutes
Cooking time 12 minutes

350g (12oz) spaghetti
salt and freshly ground black
  pepper

MEATBALLS
450g (1lb) raw lamb mince
5 tablespoons chopped fresh mint
4 tablespoons sun-dried tomato
  paste
25g (1oz) Parmesan, grated
1 small egg, beaten
1 tablespoon olive oil
2 garlic cloves, crushed
2.5cm (1in) piece fresh root ginger,
  grated
150ml (¼ pint) red wine
2 x 400g cans chopped tomatoes
1 teaspoon caster sugar

PREPARING AHEAD *Cook the meatballs and sauce in advance, and keep in the fridge for up to a day. The dish freezes well too.*

1 Put the lamb mince, 3 tablespoons of the mint, 2 tablespoons of the sun-dried tomato paste, the cheese and egg together in a bowl and mix using your hands. Season with salt and pepper and shape into 30 small balls.

2 Heat the oil in a pan, add the garlic and ginger, and fry for a minute. Add the wine, tomatoes, sugar and remaining tomato paste. Bring to the boil, then add the meatballs to the sauce. Cover and simmer for about 10 minutes or until the meatballs are cooked through.

3 Cook the spaghetti in boiling salted water for about 10 minutes, then drain and tip into a large serving dish.

4 Add the remaining mint to the sauce, check the seasoning, and pour the sauce and meatballs over the spaghetti.

5 Serve with Greek yoghurt and dressed salad leaves.

GOOD THINGS TO KNOW *If you use a lot of grated Parmesan, grate it ahead, not too finely, and freeze in a plastic container just large enough to take the quantity. Then you can help yourself when you need it, as there's no need to thaw first.*

AND ANOTHER THING *If you haven't any fresh mint, use 3 tablespoons mint sauce from a jar.*

AGA At step 2 bring the sauce and meatballs to the boil on the boiling plate, then cover and transfer to the simmering oven for about 15 minutes or until the meatballs are cooked.

Penne with Mascarpone, Fennel and Broccoli (V)

A brilliant lunch or supper dish, as nothing could be simpler. Just serve with good warm bread.

SERVES 4

Preparation time 5 minutes
Cooking time 12 minutes

300g (10oz) penne pasta
salt and freshly ground black
    pepper
1 large fennel bulb, halved, core
    removed, thinly sliced
225g (8oz) broccoli, cut into small
    florets
1 x 250g tub mascarpone cheese
1-2 garlic cloves, crushed
75g (3oz) Parmesan, grated
a small bunch of fresh basil,
    roughly chopped

PREPARING AHEAD *All the vegetables can be prepared ahead, and kept in the fridge.*

1 Cook the penne in boiling salted water for about 10-12 minutes altogether, adding the fennel after about 5 minutes.

2 Add the broccoli florets to the pasta 2 minutes before the end of the cooking time.

3 Drain the pasta and vegetables into a colander.

4 Put the mascarpone, garlic and Parmesan into the empty hot pan, and bring up to the boil, stirring.

5 Add the drained pasta and vegetables to the sauce, season well and toss in the basil. Serve at once.

GOOD THINGS TO KNOW *Fennel is an excellent vegetable that tastes of aniseed when raw. When cooked, however, the flavour changes, and is much milder. When roasting fennel wedges, always par-cook first in boiling water until almost tender. A quick roast thereafter, and the fennel will be delicious.*

Pesto Pasta Pronto (V)

Just seven ingredients, prepared, cooked and on the table in under 20 minutes.

SERVES 4-6
Preparation time 5 minutes
Cooking time 12 minutes

1 large Spanish onion, roughly
    chopped
225g (8oz) penne pasta
salt and freshly ground black
    pepper
25g (1oz) pine nuts
12 peppadew mild spicy peppers
    from a jar
3 tablespoons green pesto
50g (2oz) Parmesan, coarsely
    grated or shavings
lots of fresh parsley, chopped

1 Plunge the onion and pasta into boiling salted water, bring to the boil, and simmer for about 10-12 minutes – check the packet instructions.

2 Whilst the pasta is cooking very slowly toast the nuts in a dry pan until golden brown – watch them like a hawk – and slice the peppers into thin strips.

3 Drain the pasta and onion, return to the pan, and add the peppers, pesto and Parmesan. Season with salt and pepper, and add the chopped parsley.

4 Tip into a serving dish, scatter with the toasted pine nuts, and serve immediately.

GOOD THINGS TO KNOW *You can use green or red pesto for this recipe. Home-made pesto is delicious, but I do think the jars sold in supermarkets are very good too. Keep in the fridge after opening and if a little dry pour some more olive oil over the top of the pesto to prevent it from going mouldy.*

Fresh Asparagus and Tarragon Spaghetti (V)

*A lovely fresh and fast vegetarian dish, which is full of flavour. Just serve with
a dressed green salad.*

SERVES 4
Preparation time 5 minutes
Cooking time 12 minutes

225g (8oz) spaghetti
salt and freshly ground black
   pepper
225g (8oz) fresh asparagus tips
2 tablespoons olive oil
3 small courgettes, sliced into thin
   batons
1 x 200ml tub crème fraîche
50g (2oz) Parmesan, grated
juice of ½ lemon
2 tablespoons chopped fresh
   tarragon

TO SERVE
25g (1oz) Parmesan, grated

PREPARING AHEAD *You can
prepare the vegetables ahead,
and keep them in the fridge.*

1 Cook the spaghetti in boiling salted water for about 7 minutes, then add the asparagus tips and continue to cook for a further 3 minutes. Drain.

2 Heat the oil in a large non-stick frying pan, and fry the courgette batons over a high heat for about 2-3 minutes, or until slightly tinged with colour around the edges.

3 Add the remaining ingredients to the frying pan. Bring to the boil and stir in the hot pasta and asparagus tips. Season well with salt and pepper.

4 Mix together, tip into a warm serving dish and sprinkle with Parmesan.

GOOD THINGS TO KNOW *If the asparagus tips
are longer than 5cm (2in), cut the stalk end into slices
and cook with the spaghetti from the start, adding
the end tips for the last 3 minutes of cooking time as
suggested in the recipe.*

Spaghetti Bolognaise

Traditionally the meat is browned first, which takes time. Now you can buy really lean, good-quality beef, I find that I can do this all-in-one sauce method which takes just 10 minutes to prepare. Sometimes carrots are added, but I prefer mushrooms.

SERVES 6
Preparation time 10 minutes
Cooking time 30 minutes

400g (14 oz) spaghetti
salt and freshly ground black
   pepper
freshly grated Parmesan to serve

BOLOGNAISE SAUCE

750g (1 ¾ lb) good-quality raw,
   lean minced beef
75g (3oz) pancetta, snipped into
   small pieces
2 large onions, finely chopped
3 fat garlic cloves, crushed
150ml (¼ pint) red or white wine
2 x 400g cans chopped tomatoes
4 tablespoons tomato purée
3 tablespoons good redcurrant
   jelly
150g (5oz) small chestnut
   mushrooms, sliced
a dash of gravy browning, if liked

PREPARING AHEAD *It's a good idea to make double the quantity of sauce at one time, and freeze it, well in advance.*

1 Put the minced beef into a large pan and mash with a fork. Add the pancetta, onion, garlic and wine, and stir again to break up the meat. Add the remaining sauce ingredients, and stir well.

2 Bring to the boil, then season with salt and pepper. Cover with a lid and simmer over a low heat for about 30 minutes until thickened slightly, the meat is cooked through and the onion is tender.

3 When ready to serve, cook the spaghetti in boiling salted water as directed on the packet, about 10-12 minutes. Drain.

4 Serve the pasta with the sauce and grated Parmesan.

GOOD THINGS TO KNOW *Pancetta is unsmoked bacon preserved with a sweet cure. If you have difficulty in finding it use lean unsmoked bacon. Little packets of pre-cut pancetta lardons are now available in supermarkets.*

AGA After step 1, bring to the boil on the boiling plate, cover with a lid, and transfer to the simmering oven for about 45 minutes or until the onions are tender and the meat is cooked.

Spring Green Tagliatelle

A wonderful combination of flavours. Dried pasta is traditionally used in Italy, its great advantage being that it keeps well on the shelf, ready to use for a quick supper. I never use fresh pasta for pasta recipes.

SERVES 4

Preparation time 5 minutes
Cooking time 12 minutes

300g (10oz) dried tagliatelle pasta
1 large leek, finely sliced
salt and freshly ground black
  pepper
175g (6oz) frozen petits pois
300ml (½ pint) double cream
225g (8oz) good-quality ham, cut
  into 1cm (½in) pieces
75g (3oz) Parmesan, grated
3 tablespoons chopped fresh mint

1 Cook the tagliatelle and leek together in a pan of boiling salted water for about 12 minutes. About 2 minutes before the end of cooking, add the petits pois and continue to boil. Drain.

2 Pour the double cream into the empty pasta pan, add the ham and bring to the boil. Season with salt and pepper and add 50g (2oz) of the Parmesan and half the mint.

3 Return the tagliatelle, leeks and peas to the pan, stir and bring to the boil. Pour into a serving dish and sprinkle over the remaining Parmesan and mint.

GOOD THINGS TO KNOW *'Prosciutto' translates from Italian into English as 'ham', but what is always meant is 'prosciutto crudo', which means dry cured raw ham. Buy it from delis freshly sliced or in vacuum packs from the supermarket, usually as Parma ham from Italy (but British dry cured ham is also available, as is Serrano from Spain and Black Forest from Germany).*

Andalucian Pasta

The sauce for this pasta is more southern Mediterranean in style than specifically Italian. Not only does it use Spanish chorizo, but it includes rosemary, which gives a wonderful fresh flavour. Fusilli pasta is spiral-shaped dried pasta, and you can find packets in all supermarkets. If you can get pitted black olives in olive oil, they are far superior to those in brine.

SERVES 4

Preparation time 5 minutes
Cooking time 10 minutes

300g (10oz) fusilli pasta
salt and freshly ground black
    pepper
2 x 70g packets thin slices Spanish
    chorizo, cut in half
1 red pepper, seeded and cut into
    2.5cm (1in) cubes
2 garlic cloves, crushed
1 x 500g carton tomato passata
2 tablespoons chopped fresh
    rosemary
50g (2oz) pitted black olives,
    halved

1 Cook the fusilli in boiling salted water for about 10 minutes. Drain.

2 Fry the chorizo in a large non-stick frying pan until crisp around the edges. Add the pepper cubes and continue to fry for a few moments. Add the garlic and tomato passata, bring to the boil, and season with salt and pepper.

3 Stir in the rosemary and olives, and return the pasta to the pan. Bring back to the boil, stirring.

4 Pour into a warm serving dish and serve piping hot.

GOOD THINGS TO KNOW *Tomato passata can be bought in cartons or bottles, and is puréed tomatoes – lovely and smooth, unlike canned tomatoes which have bits in. If you cannot get passata, use 1 x 400g can chopped tomatoes.*

AND ANOTHER THING *Chorizo is a strong dry cured sausage from Spain, not unlike salami. Always buy good-quality chorizo – the price should be your guide.*

Summer Risotto (V)

This is a vegetarian risotto. If you want a meaty one, add 150g (5oz) of bacon lardons, fried until crisp, at the end.

SERVES 6

Preparation time 10 minutes
Cooking time 35 minutes

2 tablespoons olive oil
1 large onion, chopped
2 garlic cloves, crushed
2 red peppers, seeded and cut
　　into 2.5cm (1in) cubes
150ml (¼ pint) white wine
350g (12oz) risotto rice
about 900 ml (1 ½ pints) hot
　　vegetable stock
350g (12oz) cherry tomatoes,
　　halved
1 tablespoon honey
1 tablespoon balsamic vinegar
1 x 50g bag rocket, roughly
　　chopped
50g (2oz) Parmesan, shaved

1 Heat 1 tablespoon of the oil in a deep non-stick frying pan. Add the onion, garlic and peppers, and fry over a high heat for a few minutes.

2 Add the wine and boil over a high heat until it has evaporated by half. Add the rice and, stirring continuously, gradually add the boiling stock. Cook for about 20 minutes until nearly all the liquid has been absorbed and the rice is soft and creamy, stirring occasionally.

3 Just before the rice is cooked, add the tomatoes, honey, vinegar and rocket, and season well.

4 Serve hot with shavings of Parmesan.

GOOD THINGS TO KNOW Parmesan shavings are quite simple to do. Simply pull a potato peeler down the sides of a block of fresh Parmesan – it will peel off in shavings.

AGA Start the risotto on the boiling plate, then move over to the simmering plate.

Fresh Salmon and Dill Rice Bowl

This delicious combination of salmon and rice is perfect eaten in a bowl. Be sure to use fresh dill, as it makes all the difference.

SERVES 4

Preparation time 5 minutes
Cooking time 12 minutes

600ml (1 pint) water
300ml (½ pint) white wine
350g (12oz) risotto rice
8 spring onions, finely sliced
1 fennel bulb, cored and finely
  sliced
salt and freshly ground black
  pepper
500g (1lb 2oz) fresh salmon fillets,
  skinned
a large bunch of fresh dill,
  chopped
juice of 1 small lemon
25g (1oz) butter

1 Measure the water, wine, rice, white parts of the spring onions, the fennel and 1 teaspoon salt into a large saucepan. Bring to the boil, cover and simmer for about 5 minutes or until the rice is starting to soften. Stir once.

2 Place the salmon fillets on top of the rice, cover and continue to cook over a low heat for a further 6-7 minutes or until the salmon is cooked and the rice is tender.

3 Remove the salmon from the pan, and drain off any liquid from the rice. Stir the dill, lemon juice and butter into the rice. Check the seasoning. Flake the fish and stir into the rice. Serve hot.

GOOD THINGS TO KNOW

Risotto rice, a short-grained rice which is grown in the north of Italy, comes in several types, the most familiar of which is arborio. Two others are carnaroli and vialone nano, and most good supermarkets and Italian delis stock packets of at least one of them.

AND ANOTHER THING *Lucy Young, who has worked with me for yonks, will never allow me to add peas to rice, but when she's not looking I would happily add 50g (2oz) peas to this recipe, just before the salmon is added!*

Pasta with Prawns, Peppers and a hint of Chilli

This is good for a family supper. If you have surplus smoked salmon, add 150g (5oz) of finely chopped smoked salmon instead of the prawns.

SERVES 4-6

Preparation time 5 minutes
Cooking time 10 minutes

350g (12oz) fusilli pasta
salt and freshly ground black
    pepper
1-2 fresh red chillies, seeded and
    finely chopped
2 fat garlic cloves, crushed
4 tablespoons olive oil
150ml (¼ pint) double cream
2 whole red peppers in oil from a
    jar, sliced into 2.5cm (1in) strips
2 spring onions, sliced on the
    diagonal
350g (12oz) king prawns, cooked
    without shell
finely grated zest and juice of
    1 ½ lemons
a large bunch of fresh flat-leaf
    parsley, chopped
75g (3oz) Parmesan, coarsely
    grated

1 Cook the pasta in plenty of boiling salted water according to the packet instructions. Drain well.

2 Fry the chilli and garlic in the oil over a high heat for a moment, then add the cream, peppers, spring onions, prawns and seasoning. Bring to the boil and toss over the drained pasta with the lemon zest and juice and the chopped parsley.

3 Serve at once with grated Parmesan and a dressed green salad.

GOOD THINGS TO KNOW *Skinned red peppers in oil in a jar are perfect for this recipe, especially if time is short. Once open keep the jar in the fridge. Alternatively you can cook fresh peppers in a hot oven until the skin is blackened. While hot pop into a plastic bag and seal the top for the peppers to sweat. Once cold the skin will peel off easily and cut flesh into thin strips.*

Fast Lasagne al Forno with Spinach

This makes a real change from the classic lasagne, and it's so much quicker. There's no béchamel sauce, just crème fraîche instead, and the tomato sauce doesn't have to be cooked first. You will think that you haven't enough sauce for three layers but there is – don't mix the two together in layers, blob them on top at random.

SERVES 6

Preparation time 15 minutes
Cooking time 30 minutes

6 sheets, about 75g (3 oz), quick-cook white lasagne, or fresh lasagne
50g (2 oz) strong Cheddar, grated

RAGÙ AND SPINACH SAUCE

1 tablespoon olive oil
450g (1lb) pork sausagemeat
1 red chilli, seeded and finely chopped
2 fat garlic cloves, crushed
150g (5oz) button mushrooms, sliced
1x 200ml carton full-fat crème fraîche
100g (4 oz) baby spinach, roughly chopped
salt and freshly ground black pepper

TOMATO AND THYME SAUCE

1 x 400g can chopped tomatoes
2 tablespoons sun-dried tomato paste
1 teaspoon demerara sugar
1 tablespoon fresh thyme leaves

Preheat the oven to 200ºC/
Fan 180ºC/Gas 6. You will need an ovenproof dish about 1.8 litres (3 pints) in capacity, 15 x 25 x 5cm (6 x 10 x 2in).

1 For the ragù and spinach sauce, heat the oil in a large non-stick frying pan, then add the sausagemeat and brown over a high heat until golden, breaking it up with two wooden spoons.

2 Add the chilli, garlic and mushrooms and fry for a few minutes. Stir in the crème fraîche and spinach. Bring to the boil for a couple of minutes, season well and set aside.

3 To make the tomato sauce, measure all the ingredients into a jug and season well.

4 Divide the ragù sauce into thirds, and spoon a third into the base of the dish. Spoon a third of the tomato sauce on top at random, and arrange half the pasta sheets over the tomato sauce. Repeat using two more layers each of the ragù and tomato sauces and one of pasta. Sprinkle over the grated cheese.

5 Bake in the preheated oven for about 20-30 minutes or until golden brown, bubbling around the edges, and the pasta is tender.

GOOD THINGS TO KNOW *If using dried lasagne sheets, I always try to do the preparation ahead, either in the morning for supper or the night before. This gives time for the sauces to soften the pasta before cooking.*

PREPARING AHEAD *The whole dish can be prepared a day ahead and kept in the fridge. It would freeze raw as well, but thaw thoroughly before baking.*

AGA Slide on to the third set of runners in the roasting oven for about 20-30 minutes or until golden brown, bubbling around the edges, and the pasta is tender.

Fast Pasta Sauces

Double Tomato Sauce (V) Fry a medium chopped onion in a little olive oil until tender, then add a tablespoon plain flour and blend well. Stir in 1 x 400g can chopped tomatoes, 2 crushed garlic cloves, 2 tablespoons sun-dried tomato paste and 1 x 500ml carton passata. Stir well, bring to the boil, then add a little Worcestershire sauce, 2 teaspoons caster sugar and some salt and pepper. Serve with 350g (12oz) cooked pasta, adding a few chopped black olives and plenty of fresh basil to serve. Serves 4-6.

Simply Scrummy Parmesan Sauce (V) Measure 150ml (¼ pint) double cream into a pan with 2 tablespoons grated Parmesan, 1 tablespoon Dijon mustard and 2 tablespoons chopped fresh parsley. Bring to the boil, season with salt and pepper, and serve with pasta, grilled or pan-fried chicken breast, or with lightly cooked cauliflower and broccoli. Serves up to 4.

Parma Ham and Mushroom Sauce Quite our most favourite sauce with pasta. Snip a packet of dry cured ham into small pieces and lightly fry in a non-stick frying pan with 150g (5oz) sliced button mushrooms. Add a 200ml carton full-fat crème fraîche, season well with pepper and a little salt, and serve with 250g (9oz) cooked pasta and shavings of Parmesan. Serves 4.

Pesto, Olive and Tomato Sauce (V) Simply toss 350g (12oz) hot cooked pasta with 3 tablespoons olive oil, 3 tablespoons pesto, 12 chopped black olives (those in oil are best), and 4 tablespoons chopped sun-dried tomatoes. Add plenty of chopped fresh parsley. Season with salt and pepper and serve with grated Parmesan. Serves 4.

Spinach, Garlic and Pine Nut Sauce (V) Cook 350g (12oz) spaghetti, and drain. In the same pan add 1 tablespoon good olive oil, and fry 1 large chopped onion with 2 crushed garlic cloves until soft. Add 225g (8oz) spinach, finely chopped, allow to wilt, then add a further 2 tablespoons olive oil. Return the pasta to the pan, and season with salt and pepper. Serve hot with a good generous sprinkling of Parmesan and toasted pine nuts. Serves 4-6.

CHAPTER 5
VEGETARIAN, VEGETABLES AND SALADS

This chapter is a mixture of different types of vegetable recipes: some are for vegetable-based main dishes in their own right, some make delicious and unusual main courses for non-meat eaters, and some are dishes which would be perfect as an accompaniment to meat, poultry or fish. They can be hot or cold, and I have also included some main-course and accompanying salads.

We are very lucky now in that we have a marvellous selection of vegetables to buy, whether in individual shops or in supermarkets. I always try to buy in season, not only because the vegetables are better then, but because they are more reasonable too. And look out for farm shops and farmers' markets, as the vegetables will probably be as fresh as paint – and perhaps more unusual than you might find elsewhere, as smaller farmers can experiment with growing plants that might not suit the bulk demands of supermarkets.

I have given here several ways in which to stir-fry vegetables, several ways in which to use root vegetables, and quite a few suggestions as to how you can vary both your basic mashed potato and baked potato recipes. Often, to make a more substantial vegetable recipe, you can add something like pastry – as a base or as a wrapping – and here I have made some little tarts with an unusual scone base. There are a couple of recipes here which are classics, but, once again, I have given them a little twist.

All the recipes here are quite fast, but many of them can actually be prepared ahead. I often prepare vegetables themselves beforehand. Potatoes and carrots can be peeled in advance, for instance, and will happily sit in water until you need them.

Baked Aubergine with Raclette Cheese (V)

'Parmigiano di melanzane' is a classic Italian dish, but one which is rarely made at home. In Italy it is usually made with fried aubergine, but my version, using blanched aubergine slices, is much lighter.

SERVES 4-6

Preparation time 15 minutes
Cooking time 20 minutes

2 medium aubergines
salt and freshly ground black
    pepper
100g (4oz) raclette cheese, cut
    into thin slices
40g (1 ½oz) Parmesan, freshly
    grated

TOMATO SAUCE

1 tablespoon olive oil
1 large onion, chopped
2 fat garlic cloves, crushed
1 x 500g carton tomato passata
a pinch of caster sugar
1 tablespoon chopped fresh basil

Preheat the oven to 200°C/
Fan 180°C/Gas 6.

PREPARING AHEAD *Prepare it all the day before, apart from sprinkling with Parmesan. Bake straight from the fridge, sprinkling with the Parmesan at the last minute.*

1 First make the tomato sauce. Measure the oil into a frying pan, add the onion, cover and cook over a low heat for about 10 minutes or until soft. Add the garlic, tomato passata, sugar, salt and pepper and basil, and bring to the boil. Remove from the heat.

2 Meanwhile, trim the stalks from the aubergines and slice into thin slices. Cook in a little boiling salted water for about 5 minutes until soft but still holding their shape. Drain and pat dry on kitchen paper.

3 Pour half the tomato sauce into an ovenproof dish of about 25 x 22cm (10 x 8 ½in). Lay half the aubergines on top, and season. Place the slices of raclette cheese on top of the aubergine. Lay the remaining slices of aubergine on top of the cheese, and pour over the remaining tomato sauce.

4 Sprinkle with Parmesan and bake in the preheated oven for about 20 minutes until bubbling and the cheese has browned. Serve hot.

GOOD THINGS TO KNOW *Raclette is a semi-hard cheese used for a Swiss speciality known by the same name. Half a large raclette cheese is put in front of an open fire, and the melted surface is scraped off and eaten with potatoes, pickled onions and gherkins. If you can't get raclette, use Emmental or Gruyère.*

AGA Slide the dish on to the top set of runners in the roasting oven for about 15-20 minutes.

Plum Tomato and Thyme Galettes (V)

These are delicious served hot with a dressed salad. I have used a scone base rather than pastry as a change, as it is very quick to do. The dough can actually be made in a processor if time is short.

SERVES 6

Preparation time 15 minutes
Cooking time 25 minutes

2 tablespoons olive oil
1 large onion, finely sliced
6 plum tomatoes, thinly sliced
leaves from 12 sprigs fresh thyme
salt and freshly ground black
   pepper
a little balsamic vinegar

SCONE BASE

175g (6oz) self-raising flour
75g (3oz) butter, cubed
½ teaspoon dry English mustard
50g (2oz) Cheddar, grated
2 tablespoons green pesto
1 egg, beaten, made up to 75ml
   (⅛ pint) with milk

Preheat the oven to 200°C/
Fan 180°C/Gas 6, and put a
baking sheet in it to get very hot.

1 Heat 1 tablespoon of the oil in a non-stick frying pan, add the onion, cover and simmer over a low heat for about 10 minutes or until soft.

2 To make the scone base, measure the flour and butter into a mixing bowl, and rub together using your hands until it looks like fine breadcrumbs. Stir in the mustard, cheese and pesto, and gradually add the egg liquid until the dough comes together and is soft and fairly sticky.

3 Roll the dough out on a floured surface until about 5mm (¼ in) thick. Cut out six rounds about 11cm (4 ¼in) in diameter, using a scone cutter (or cut around a saucer). You may need to re-roll the dough once more to get the sixth round.

4 Spread the drained onion over the rounds, and arrange the tomato slices over the top, overlapping slightly. Sprinkle over the thyme leaves and some salt and pepper. Drizzle a tiny amount of oil and balsamic vinegar over the tomatoes.

5 Sit the galettes on the piping hot baking sheet and bake in the preheated oven for about 25 minutes, or until the scone base is cooked and golden brown underneath. Serve warm.

GOOD THINGS TO KNOW *It is important to preheat the baking sheet, as this will ensure the scone is cooked from underneath, and is brown and not soggy.*

AGA No need to heat the baking sheet, cook on the floor of the roasting oven for about 20 minutes.

Char-grilled Vegetable Strudel with Roquefort (V)

You can use any cheese in this recipe, but we like Roquefort best. If you have any leftover cheese from a cheeseboard, e.g. Stilton or mature Cheddar, you can use this as well, but it is important to use a cheese with a strong flavour.

SERVES 6
Preparation time 15 minutes
Cooking time 25 minutes

6 sheets filo pastry
50g (2oz) butter, melted
75g (3oz) Roquefort cheese, sliced

CHAR-GRILLED VEGETABLES

1 onion, sliced into thin wedges
1 small aubergine, cut in half
  lengthways and cut into thin
  slices
2 red peppers, seeded and cut
  into 2.5cm (1in) pieces
2 courgettes, trimmed and cut into
  2.5cm (1in) slices
3 tablespoons olive oil
salt and freshly ground black
  pepper

Preheat the oven to 200°C/
Fan 180°C/Gas 6. Preheat a
baking sheet to get very hot.

PREPARING AHEAD *Make the whole strudel first thing in the morning for lunch, or at lunchtime for an evening meal.*

1 Mix the prepared vegetables together with the oil in a poly bag or bowl, and toss so they are evenly coated. Sprinkle with salt and pepper.

2 Heat a non-stick ridged grill pan or large frying pan until very hot, then char-grill the vegetables in batches until they are coloured and tender. Set aside to cool.

3 Place 2 filo pastry sheets lengthways on a work surface so they are slightly overlapping, to make a rectangle measuring about 35 x 33cm (14 x 13in). Brush with melted butter, then place another 2 sheets on top widthways, again slightly overlapping. Repeat with another layer, brushing with butter in between.

4 Spoon the cooled char-grilled vegetables over the bottom third of the pastry about 7.5cm (3in) from the edge and 5cm (2in) from the sides. Arrange the cheese over the roasted vegetables.

5 Fold the base and the sides of the pastry in, and roll up to a sausage shape. Brush the strudel with melted butter.

6 Carefully transfer to the baking sheet in the preheated oven and bake for about 20-25 minutes or until golden brown and crisp on top and underneath.

7 Serve hot in slices with dressed green salad and garlic bread.

GOOD THINGS TO KNOW *This has become one of our firm favourites for lunch – just serve with a dressed salad. Sometimes we use different quantities of the*

individual vegetables so long as the total weight is about 1kg (2 ¼lb). You can use anything that is in the fridge. If you are using frozen filo, which is inexpensive, always thaw it first, either overnight in the fridge, or at room temperature for about 6 hours.

AGA No need to preheat a baking sheet. Slide the strudel on a cold baking sheet directly on to the floor of the roasting oven for about 25 minutes or until the pastry is golden and crisp underneath.

Cannelloni alla Sorrentina (V)

Quite a classic cannelloni recipe, but it is very fast to make. If you can't get fresh lasagne, cook some dried, then roll up. If Roquefort is unavailable, use any other blue cheese.

SERVES 4
Preparation time 10 minutes
Cooking time 30 minutes

8 fresh lasagne sheets

TOMATO SAUCE
1 tablespoon olive oil
1 red chilli, seeded and finely
  chopped
2 garlic cloves, crushed
2 x 400g cans chopped tomatoes
1 teaspoon caster sugar
salt and freshly ground black
  pepper

CHEESE FILLING
250g (9oz) fresh baby spinach,
  roughly chopped
1 egg, beaten
250g (9oz) ricotta cheese
100g (4oz) Roquefort cheese,
  diced
1 tablespoon Dijon mustard
6 spring onions, sliced
150g (5oz) mozzarella cheese,
  grated

Preheat the oven to 200°C/
Fan 180°C/Gas 6. You will need
a 2.2 litre (4 pint) shallow ovenproof
dish, just large enough to take
eight cannelloni rolls in a single
layer.

PREPARING AHEAD *Prepare
entirely the day before, cover and
store in the fridge. Bake from the
fridge.*

1 First make the tomato sauce. Heat the oil in a large non-stick frying pan. Add the chilli and garlic and fry over a high heat for about 30 seconds, being careful not to burn, stirring. Add the tomatoes and sugar, bring to the boil, season with salt and pepper, and simmer over a low heat, uncovered, for about 5 minutes.

2 To make the filling, heat a non-stick pan until very hot. Add the spinach and stir-fry until just wilted. Season with salt and pepper, and drain off any liquid if necessary.
Add the remaining filling ingredients to the egg, except for a quarter of the mozzarella cheese, and stir in the spinach.

3 Arrange the lasagne sheets in a small bowl, pour over boiling water to cover, and leave to soften for about 3-4 minutes. Drain and refresh in cold water.

4 Arrange the softened sheets of lasagne on the work surface. Divide the cheese mixture between the sheets, and roll up lengthways.

5 Spoon a quarter of the tomato sauce into the base of the shallow ovenproof dish, and arrange the cannelloni on top of the tomato, seam-side down. Pour over the remaining tomato sauce and sprinkle with the remaining mozzarella.

6 Bake in the preheated oven for about 25-30 minutes or until golden brown and hot in the middle, and the pasta is tender.

GOOD THINGS TO KNOW *Adding mustard to a cheese sauce helps to bring out the flavour of the cheese.*

AGA Slide the ovenproof dish on to the second set of runners in the roasting oven for about 10 minutes. Slide the grid shelf on to the floor of the roasting oven and cook for a further 15-20 minutes.

Creamy Vegetable Curry (V)

Unlike some curries, this is very quick to prepare and cook. It has more of a Thai influence than an Indian. With other curries, and rice, it could make a good meal for a non-meat eater.

SERVES 6

Preparation time 10 minutes
Cooking time 20 minutes

1 tablespoon sunflower oil
1 large onion, roughly chopped
1 fresh red chilli, seeded and finely chopped
5cm (2in) piece fresh root ginger, peeled and finely grated
2-3 tablespoons medium curry powder
1 tablespoon ground turmeric
2 x 400g cans chopped tomatoes
600ml (1 pint) chicken or vegetable stock
350g (12oz) carrots, cut into 2.5cm (1in) batons
350g (12oz) new potatoes, halved lengthways
350g (12oz) cauliflower, cut into small florets
1 x 200ml carton coconut cream (UHT)
salt and freshly ground black pepper

PREPARING AHEAD *Can be made the day before, but add the cauliflower florets when reheating the dish.*

1 Heat the oil in a large, deep non-stick frying pan. Add the onion, chilli, ginger and spices, and fry over a high heat for about 2-3 minutes.

2 Add the tomatoes and their juices, the stock, carrots and potatoes. Cover with a lid, bring to the boil and simmer over a low heat for about 15 minutes.

3 Remove the lid, and add the cauliflower florets and coconut cream. Season with salt and pepper and boil for a further 5 minutes, uncovered, until all the vegetables are cooked and the sauce has thickened.

4 Check the seasoning, and serve hot.

GOOD THINGS TO KNOW *Coconut cream can be bought in a carton, and is thick like single cream. If you can only buy coconut milk, use a 400g can and reduce the stock quantity to 300ml (½ pint).*

AGA Fry step 1 on the boiling plate. Continue with step 2, bring to the boil, cover and transfer to the simmering oven for about 15 minutes. Remove the lid and continue as above on the boiling plate.

Baked Potatoes with Bacon, Avocado and Mozzarella

Large potatoes are best for this dish, e.g. King Edward, Désirée or Maris Piper. Choose an avocado that is firm but just ripe. Serve the stuffed baked potatoes with a dressed green salad.

SERVES 4

Preparation time 10 minutes
Cooking time 1½ hours

4 large main-crop potatoes

FILLING

100g (4oz) streaky bacon, snipped, or bacon lardons
a little butter or milk
1 avocado
salt and freshly ground black pepper
75g (3oz) mozzarella cheese, grated
a little paprika

Preheat the oven to 220°C/ Fan 200°C/Gas 7.

PREPARING AHEAD *The potatoes can be baked ahead, either the day before for lunch, or in the morning for supper.*

1 Bake the potatoes in the preheated oven for about 1 ¼ hours until cooked through and crisp. If you are in a hurry, cut them in half before baking and they will then only take about 45 minutes.

2 Meanwhile, fry the bacon pieces in a non-stick pan until crisp and brown. Drain well.

3 Remove the potatoes from the oven and leave to cool. Cut in half and scoop the potato flesh out into a bowl, keeping the shells intact. Mash the potato until smooth with a little butter or milk.

4 Halve and remove the stone from the avocado. Skin and cut into small pieces the size of large peas.

5 Mix the bacon, avocado and some salt and pepper into the mash. Spoon the mash mixture back into the potato shells, and sprinkle over the mozzarella and paprika.

6 Arrange the filled potatoes in a buttered roasting tin or dish and return to the oven for about 15 minutes until golden brown and heated through.

GOOD THINGS TO KNOW *You can vary this recipe with some alternative fillings. Omit the bacon, avocado and mozzarella.*

Hummus and Haloumi Cheese *Mix a 200g tub of hummus with the mash, and season with salt and pepper. Spoon back into the potato shells and top with about 75g (3oz) grated haloumi cheese.*

Mango Chutney and Cheddar *Mix 2 tablespoons mango chutney with the mash, stir in 3 finely sliced spring onions, and season with salt and pepper. Spoon back into the potato shells and top with about 75g (3oz) grated Cheddar.*

Bacon, Mustard and Cheddar *Mix about 100g (4oz) crispy bacon lardons with the mash, stir in 2 tablespoons grainy mustard and season with salt and pepper. Spoon back into the potato shells and top with about 75g (3oz) grated Cheddar.*

AGA For the first stage, roast the potatoes on the top set of runners in the roasting oven for about an hour or until cooked through and crisp. For the baking of the stuffed potatoes, cook at the top of the roasting oven for a slightly shorter time.

Herby Tabbouleh (V)

Make sure that this is well seasoned, with the flavours of the lemon and olive oil foremost. Tabbouleh should be bright, bright green from the herbs, and you should hardly be able to see the wheat at all.

SERVES 6 AS A SIDE SALAD
Preparation time 12 minutes

225g (8oz) bulgar wheat
finely grated zest and juice of 2
  lemons
6 bunch of spring onions, finely
  sliced
1 large bunches fresh mint, roughly
  chopped
1 large bunch fresh flat-leaf
  parsley, roughly chopped
2 tablespoons extra virgin olive oil
1 cucumber, peeled, deseeded
  and cut into 1cm (½in) cubes
salt and freshly ground black
  pepper

PREPARING AHEAD *Make the bulk of the salad a couple of hours in advance, but do not add the cucumber until the last moment, otherwise it will become soft and make the salad too wet.*

1 Measure the bulgar wheat into a saucepan, and cover with water. Bring to the boil and gently boil for about 10-12 minutes until soft. Drain, refresh in cold water and drain well again.

2 Tip the bulgar wheat into a bowl and mix in the remaining ingredients. Season well with salt and pepper.

GOOD THINGS TO KNOW *Bulgar wheat, also known as burghul, bulgur or cracked wheat, is a product made by parboiling wheat, drying it, and then coarsely grinding it. Look on the packet for cooking instructions – some wheats do not need much cooking.*

Beetroot, Carrot and Sultana Salad (V)

This salad looks very pretty, and its dressing has an unusual sweet and sour flavour.

SERVES 4

Preparation time 10 minutes

500g (1lb 2oz) cooked beetroot, finely diced

1 shallot, very finely chopped

1 large carrot, peeled and cut into 1cm (½in) dice

25g (1oz) sultanas

2 tablespoons chopped fresh parsley

salt and freshly ground black pepper

DRESSING

2 tablespoons grainy mustard

2 tablespoons white wine vinegar

4 tablespoons olive oil

2 tablespoons runny honey

PREPARING AHEAD

Cook the beetroot well in advance, but prepare everything else at the last minute.

1 Mix all the ingredients for the salad, except the parsley, together in a large bowl.

2 Measure the ingredients for the dressing into a bowl and whisk to combine.

3 Pour the dressing over the salad, season with salt and pepper and sprinkle with parsley.

GOOD THINGS TO KNOW *If you are making this in the summer, and have an abundance of herbs in the garden, you could add 2 tablespoons chopped fresh coriander or chives if liked.*

Chickpea and Pesto Salad (V)

This salad is Italian inspired, and is wonderful as an accompaniment to cold meats in the summer – or by itself for non-meat eaters.

SERVES 4
Preparation time 10 minutes

1 small garlic clove, crushed
1 x 400g can chickpeas, rinsed
and drained
50g (2oz) mixed olives, pitted and
quartered
100g (4oz) feta cheese, cubed
100g (4oz) sun-blushed tomatoes,
roughly chopped
3 tablespoons chopped fresh
parsley

DRESSING
2 tablespoons balsamic vinegar
2 tablespoons green pesto
2 tablespoons olive oil
salt and freshly ground black
pepper

PREPARING AHEAD *Most of this salad can be made the day before – just add the chickpeas and dressing on the day so everything stays crisp.*

1 Measure all the ingredients for the dressing into a large bowl, seasoning well, and whisk until combined.

2 Add the remaining ingredients to the dressing, toss and season well.

GOOD THINGS TO KNOW *This salad can also be made with a can of mixed beans such as cannellini or flageolet instead of chickpeas.*

Green Salad with Pan-fried Sirloin and Horseradish dressing

This main-course salad is perfect for an impromptu lunch or supper. A 225g (8oz) sirloin steak will be about 2.5cm (1in) thick. You can serve the salad in one large bowl, or in four individual ones, as we did in the photograph. Cut the steak at the last minute, and serve on a board alongside.

SERVES 4
Preparation time 10 minutes
Cooking time 5 minutes

2 x 225g (8oz) sirloin steaks
salt and freshly ground black
 pepper

SALAD

100g (4oz) French beans, trimmed
1 little gem lettuce
3 large plum tomatoes, cut into
 wedges
1 x 85g bag watercress
1 ripe avocado
a little lemon juice

DRESSING

3 tablespoons olive oil
3 tablespoons creamy horseradish
 sauce
1 teaspoon Dijon mustard
2 tablespoons single cream

PREPARING AHEAD *Make the dressing well in advance.*

1 To prepare the salad, blanch the beans in boiling salted water for about 4-5 minutes until just tender. Drain and refresh in cold water until cold, then set aside to dry.

2 Break the little gem leaves into bite-sized pieces and arrange in a large bowl. Toss in the tomato wedges, watercress and dry beans, and season with salt and pepper.

3 Halve the avocado and remove the stone. Peel and slice both halves thickly, then toss in lemon juice. Mix into the salad.

4 Heat a non-stick frying pan over a high heat until piping hot. Cook the steak for about 2 minutes on each side (see page 74). Transfer to a plate, cover with foil, and leave to rest for about 5 minutes while making the dressing.

5 Mix all the dressing ingredients together in a small bowl, and pour half the dressing over the salad. Toss well.

6 Cut the steak into slices, and serve warm with the salad and remaining dressing.

GOOD THINGS TO KNOW *Long-life lemon juice in a bottle keeps in the fridge, and is handy to use when preventing avocado and fruit such as apples, peaches and halved grapes from turning brown through oxidisation.*

Chinese Noodle and Vegetable Stir-fry (V)

This tasty stir-fry is good to serve with grilled chops, spare ribs or fish. It can be served with something like the vegetable curry on page 146 for non-meat eaters.

SERVES 4

Preparation time 10 minutes
Cooking time 10 minutes

100g (4oz) medium egg noodles
2 tablespoons sunflower oil
2 red peppers, thinly sliced
8 spring onions, thinly sliced on the
    diagonal
2.5cm (1in) piece fresh root ginger,
    grated
225g (8oz) pak-choi, thinly sliced,
    keeping white and green parts
    separate
salt and freshly ground black
    pepper
a few salted cashew nuts

SAUCE

1 tablespoon Chinese five-spice
    powder
2 tablespoons soy sauce
2 tablespoons runny honey
1 teaspoon white wine vinegar

PREPARING AHEAD *All the vegetables can be prepared up to 12 hours ahead, covered with clingfilm and kept in the fridge. Then you stir-fry, and it will all be on the table in 10 minutes.*

1 Cook the noodles according to the packet instructions, then drain and refresh in cold water.

2 Heat the oil in a large non-stick frying pan. Add the peppers, spring onions, ginger and white parts of the pak-choi and fry over a high heat, stirring, for about 4-5 minutes until the vegetables are nearly cooked but still crisp.

3 Add the noodles and green pak-choi leaves to the pan, and heat through for a few minutes.

4 Mix the sauce ingredients together in a small bowl until smooth. Pour over the noodles in the pan and season with salt and pepper. Heat again, stirring until piping hot.

5 Sprinkle in the cashew nuts, and serve at once, with extra soy sauce if liked.

GOOD THINGS TO KNOW *Chinese egg noodles cook quickly – in about 4 minutes – and are made from wheat flour and egg, a good alternative to rice.*

French Vegetable Stir-fry (V)

This stir-fry reminds me of the French dish of peas and lettuce, which was very popular in the 1960s ! I've used spinach here, which has much more flavour than lettuce when hot. This can be an accompaniment to meats such as chops or steaks, or is lovely on its own for non-meat eaters.

SERVES 6

Preparation time 5 minutes
Cooking time 15 minutes

1 tablespoon olive oil
2 large onions, finely chopped
500g (1lb) frozen petits pois
225g (8oz) baby spinach, roughly
   chopped
3 tablespoons double cream
salt and freshly ground black
   pepper
3 tablespoons roughly chopped
   fresh mint

1 Heat the oil in a large frying pan until hot. Add the onions, cover, and cook over a low heat for about 7-10 minutes until soft. Remove the lid and drive off any moisture over a high heat.

2 Add the petits pois to the onions, and toss over a high heat for about 2 minutes until the peas are nearly cooked.

3 Add the spinach and cream, and bring to the boil. Season with salt and pepper, add the mint and serve.

GOOD THINGS TO KNOW *If you have lettuces that have gone to seed, use the under leaves instead of the spinach.*

Summer Stir-fry (V)

This is a mixture of cabbage, broad beans and mushrooms, which go very well together, and are just that little bit different. The stir-fry goes well with lamb or pork chops and steak.

SERVES 4

Preparation time 5 minutes
Cooking time 12 minutes

175g (6oz) frozen baby broad
  beans
salt and freshly ground black
  pepper
1 tablespoon sunflower oil
1 onion, thinly sliced
250g (9oz) small chestnut
  mushrooms, sliced
1 small pointed cabbage, core
  removed, leaves thinly sliced

1 Cook the broad beans in boiling salted water for about 3-5 minutes until soft, then drain and refresh in cold water.

2 Heat the oil in a large frying pan, add the onion and fry for a few minutes until tender, but without colouring.

3 Add the mushrooms and cabbage to the pan, and stir-fry over a high heat for about 4-5 minutes or until the cabbage has just wilted. Season with salt and pepper, and serve.

GOOD THINGS TO KNOW *Pointed cabbage, sometimes called sweetheart cabbage, is crisp and young. You just need to remove the core and the stalks from the outside leaves.*

Roasted English Roots (V)

These are perfect to go with any roast or any other meat main course. If you prefer, cut the vegetables in larger pieces, but of course they will take a little longer.

SERVES 4

Preparation time 10 minutes
Cooking time 20 minutes

350g (12oz) parsnips, peeled and cut into 2.5cm (1in) batons
350g (12oz) carrots, peeled and cut into 2.5cm (1in) batons
350g (12oz) potatoes, peeled and cut into 2.5cm (1in) batons
350g (12oz) butternut squash, peeled and cut into 2.5cm (1in) batons
salt and freshly ground black pepper
3 tablespoons sunflower oil
5 sprigs fresh thyme

Preheat the oven to 220°C/ Fan 200°C/Gas 7.

PREPARING AHEAD *You can roast the vegetables well in advance, but slightly undercooking them. Leave them in the roasting tin, and return to the oven for about 20 minutes before serving.*

1 Blanch the prepared vegetables in boiling salted water for about 5 minutes, then drain well.

2 Measure the oil into a large roasting tin, and heat in the preheated oven for about 3 minutes until piping hot.

3 Tip the vegetables and thyme into the hot oil, season with salt and pepper, and mix until all the vegetables are coated in the oil.

4 Roast in the oven for about 15-20 minutes or until golden brown and cooked through.

GOOD THINGS TO KNOW *You can use a variety of root vegetables in this way. Swede, turnips, pumpkin and sweet potatoes will all roast very well. The essential thing is to use a large roasting tin and space the vegetables out well. If they are piled on top of each other they will just go soggy and not become crisp.*

AND ANOTHER THING *Batons are short thick pencil strips!*

AGA Slide the roasting tin directly on to the floor of the roasting oven for about 15 minutes, turning over halfway through.

Roasted Mediterranean Vegetables with Balsamic Dressing (V)

Roasted vegetables are perfect to serve hot with a main course or, alternatively, lovely as a cold salad in their own right (see below).

SERVES 4

Preparation time 10 minutes
Cooking time 30 minutes

3 tablespoons olive oil
350g (12oz) aubergine, trimmed
    and cut into thin slices
350g (12oz) courgettes, trimmed
    and cut into 4 x 1cm (1 ½ x ½in)
    batons
2 yellow peppers, seeded and cut
    into large pieces
1 large onion, cut into thick
    wedges
2 garlic cloves, unskinned
salt and freshly ground black
    pepper
2 tablespoons balsamic vinegar

Preheat the oven to 220°C/
Fan 200°C/Gas 7.

PREPARING AHEAD *You can cook the whole lot ahead, just slightly undercooking, and keeping in the roasting tin. Reheat in the oven for about 20 minutes.*

1 Measure the oil into a large bowl. Add the prepared vegetables and garlic and toss in the oil. Season with salt and pepper.

2 Tip into a large roasting tin and roast in the preheated oven for about 30 minutes or until golden brown and just tender. Stir once halfway through cooking.

3 Peel the roasted garlic into a bowl, and mash with the back of a teaspoon to a paste. Add the balsamic vinegar to the garlic and mix together. Pour over the hot vegetables, and serve.

GOOD THINGS TO KNOW *For a delicious salad, follow the recipe as above. Add 50g (2oz) sun-blushed tomatoes, 225g (8oz) goat's cheese or buffalo mozzarella, cut into cubes, and a large bunch of basil, with its leaves torn, to the roasted vegetables. Toss well. This can be served hot, but is wonderful cold, as a salad to serve for a picnic or barbecue.*

AGA Slide the roasting tin directly on the floor of the roasting oven for about 30 minutes.

Parisienne Potatoes (V)

So often when potatoes, onion and cream are cooked together, you end up with the cream curdling. But in this recipe, because the potatoes and onions are boiled ahead, you will not have that problem. I'm afraid this is not a recipe for dieters, but you can always opt for a very small portion...

SERVES 6-8
Preparation time 10 minutes
Cooking time 15-20 minutes

1.5 kg (3 ¼lb) potatoes
1 large onion, sliced into about
   14 wedges
salt and freshly ground black
   pepper
300ml (½ pint) double cream
75g (3oz) Gruyère cheese, grated

Preheat the oven to 200°C/
Fan 180°C/Gas 6.

PREPARING AHEAD *You can do quite a lot of the dish up to 12 hours in advance. Boil the potatoes and onion, turn into the dish and season. Just before going into the oven, pour over the cream, and top with cheese. If cooking from cold, the cooking time will be about 10 minutes longer.*

1 Peel the potatoes and cut into 2.5cm (1in) cubes or thick slices.

2 Put the potatoes and onion into a pan, cover with cold salted water and boil for about 10 mins or until the potatoes are just cooked.

3 Drain and pour into a shallow buttered ovenproof dish, season with salt and pepper and pour over the cream.

4 Sprinkle with cheese and cook in the preheated oven for about 15-20 minutes or until golden brown and bubbling.

GOOD THINGS TO KNOW *Use potatoes such as Arran Pilot, Golden Wonder or King Edward, because they are not too floury, and don't break up in cooking. Don't attempt to use single cream here, because the consistency will be wrong.*

AGA Cook in the roasting oven towards the top for about 15 minutes.

Stilton Mash (v)

I think mash is my favourite way of serving potatoes – especially good with a dish served with a lot of sauce or gravy. Floury potatoes are the best to use, e.g. Désirée.

SERVES 6
Preparation time 5 minutes
Cooking time 20 minutes

900g (2lb) old potatoes
salt and freshly ground black
   pepper
about 150ml (¼ pint) hot milk
75g (3oz) Stilton cheese, coarsely
   grated
a good handful of chopped fresh
   parsley

PREPARING AHEAD *You can prepare mashes a few hours ahead of time. Cool quickly, put into a buttered shallow dish, and chill. Reheat, covered with foil, in a hot oven for about 20 minutes.*

1 Peel the potatoes, and cut into even-sized cubes. Cover with salted water in a saucepan, bring to the boil and boil for about 20 minutes until tender. Drain thoroughly.

2 Return the potatoes to the pan, draw to one side off the heat, and add the hot milk and Stilton. Return to the heat, and allow to almost boil on the hob.

3 Mash until smooth, then lighten by giving it a quick whisk with a small ball whisk. Lightly mix in the parsley and some black pepper. Serve hot.

GOOD THINGS TO KNOW *To vary the mash, leave out the Stilton and parsley.*

Bacon and Onion Mash *Add 100g (4oz) fried bacon lardons and 1 large chopped fried onion to the mashed potato with a good knob of butter.*

Fresh Herb Mash *Add 2 tablespoons fresh chopped leafy herbs and a dollop of cream.*

Spring Onion Mash *Finely chop 6 spring onions, including most of the green part, and add 4 tablespoons mayonnaise.*

Mustard and Chive Mash *Add 2 tablespoons grainy mustard, 4 tablespoons chopped chives and a good knob of butter.*

Celeriac and Potato Mash *Cook 450g (1lb) each of potatoes and celeriac together in salted water, drain and mash with a 200g carton crème fraîche (no milk) and some black pepper.*

CHAPTER 6
TEA FOR A CROWD

We open our garden annually for the National Gardens Scheme, so I am really quite practised at making tea for lots of people. We often serve scones with jam and cream, for instance, and I give my favourite recipe here. We bake the scones well in advance when we have time, and put them in bags to freeze, after which it is really no effort to defrost and refresh them on the day. We make traybakes and freeze them too, usually un-iced; because of their straightforward square or rectangular shapes, they are easy to stack in the freezer, one on top of the other. When they are defrosted, they are iced on the morning of the day itself. The same goes for brownies.

As far as cakes are concerned, I think I have come up with a unique idea: three types of cake from one basic mix. These may take time to make, but in one session you will have produced enough to feed a small army – and it will look as if you have been baking all week! Ideal for a weekend when you have guests – and defines what I think of as fast.

Sandwiches are often a basic constituent of tea, whether for a few friends or a crowd. Some varieties can be prepared ahead, and this is exactly what I do when I am expecting all those people every summer. Our open days are normally on a Sunday, so we make the sandwiches on the Saturday. We layer them very close together, wrap them well, store them in the fridge, and then cut them on the day. If you choose your fillings really carefully, you could do them perhaps two days ahead. It may seem an unusual idea but, after all, when you buy your lunchtime sandwich in the supermarket, that will have been made quite a time in advance.

Prepare-ahead Sandwiches

For lunch serve two rounds per person and for tea serve one and a half – less, if not for a hungry crowd. Serve two options of meat or fish and one vegetarian. These sandwiches can be made up to two days ahead.

Start with really fresh bread. Buy thin- or medium-sliced bread, white or brown, and 18 slices (nine rounds) makes about 36 sandwiches. Remember to season well with salt and pepper and to use butter.

Make the sandwiches, leaving the crusts on. Layer four sandwiches on top of each other on a large tray that will fit in your fridge. Cover with a layer of damp kitchen paper then wrap tightly with clingfilm, and keep the tray in the fridge.

On the day of serving remove the crusts from the sandwiches and cut into four (either triangles or rectangles). Ideally do this about 2 hours before eating. Cover with clingfilm, and keep at room temperature until serving.

Smoked Salmon

1 loaf medium-sliced brown bread
100g (4oz) butter, softened
1 x 400g packet smoked salmon slices
salt and freshly ground black pepper
lemon wedges to garnish

Cream Cheese, Rocket and Mango Chutney

1 loaf medium-sliced white bread
100g (4oz) butter, softened
225g (8oz) full-fat cream cheese
½ x 360g jar spreadable mango chutney
1 x 50g bag rocket, roughly chopped
salt and freshly ground black pepper

Egg Mayonnaise and Chives

1 loaf medium-sliced white bread
100g (4oz) butter, softened
9 eggs, hard-boiled
150ml (¼ pint) low-calorie mayonnaise
salt and freshly ground black pepper
1 large bunch fresh chives, snipped

OTHER SUGGESTIONS

Chicken liver pâté and snipped sun-blushed tomatoes
Pastrami, horseradish and lamb's lettuce
Tuna mayonnaise, diced celery and watercress
Brie, halved seedless grapes and cranberry sauce
Hummus, roasted red pepper (from a jar in oil) and rocket
Grated mature Cheddar, beetroot and romaine lettuce
Ham, cucumber with mustard mayonnaise
Crispy bacon, mozzarella cheese and basil
Prawn, tartare sauce, spring onions and avocado
Crab, curried mayonnaise and cucumber
Chicken, basil pesto and cherry tomatoes
Olive tapenade, sun-blushed tomatoes and Cambezola cheese

The Very Best Scones (v)

These are great for cream teas for a crowd. We make them for our garden open days in the summer. We make in advance, pack in bags of ten, and freeze (see below). If cost is a factor, use margarine instead of butter. Incidentally, to be correct you should break scones open, but if you are dealing with a crowd, cutting is the more sensible option. You should reckon on two halves per person.

MAKES 40

Preparation time 10 minutes
Cooking time 12 minutes

900g (2lb) self-raising flour
8 teaspoons baking powder
175g (6oz) butter, softened
100g (4oz) caster sugar
4 eggs
about 500ml (18fl oz) milk

Preheat the oven to 220°C/ Fan 200°C/Gas 7, and lightly grease two baking trays.

PREPARING AHEAD *Scones freeze very well, but we always refresh them in a warm oven before serving, after defrosting.*

1 Measure the flour and baking powder into a processor. Add the butter and process until like a crumble, then add the sugar. Or make by hand by rubbing the butter into the flour using your fingertips until the mixture resembles fine breadcrumbs. Stir in the sugar.

2 Beat the eggs together until blended and make up to a generous 600ml (1 pint) with the milk, then put about 4 tablespoons of the egg/milk aside in a cup for glazing the scones later. Gradually add the egg/milk mixture to the dry ingredients until you have a soft dough. It is far better that the scone mixture is on the wet side, sticking to your fingers, as the scones will rise better.

3 Turn the dough on to a lightly floured surface and flatten it out with your hand, or use a rolling pin, to a thickness of 1-2cm (½-¾in). Use a 5cm (2in) fluted cutter to stamp out the dough by pushing the cutter straight down into the dough (as opposed to twisting the cutter) then lifting it straight out. This ensures that the scones will rise evenly and keep their shape. Gently push the remaining dough together, knead very lightly then re-roll and cut more scones out as before.

4 Arrange the scones on the prepared baking trays and brush the tops with the reserved beaten egg/milk mixture to glaze. Bake in the preheated oven for about 10-15 minutes or until the scones are well risen

and golden. Cool on a wire rack, covered with a clean tea-towel to keep them moist.

5 Serve as fresh as possible, cut in half and spread both halves generously with strawberry jam. Top with a good spoonful of thick cream.

GOOD THINGS TO KNOW *As far as amounts of jam and cream for numbers are concerned, you will need about 1.3kg (3lb) jam and 900ml (1 ½ pints) cream for 40 scones.*

AND ANOTHER THING *To make brown scones, use wholemeal self-raising flour instead of white. You may need to use more liquid as the brown flour is more absorbent.*

AGA Bake on the grid shelf on the floor of the roasting oven for about 8 minutes and then directly on the floor for a further 5-7 minutes until golden brown and risen.

Mary's garden

Fast Baking – Make Three Cakes at One Go (V)

I was asked to do this for a recent TV programme – to make 3 completely different types of cake from one basic cake mix: a superb chocolate cake, a lemon drizzle loaf cake and a dozen almond fruity buns. It's such a good and time-saving idea, especially when you have several friends to visit, perhaps over the weekend. The cakes could be baked in the oven at the same time if your oven is large, or baked in batches.

SERVES ABOUT 12 FOR A TEA (the chocolate cake cuts into 8, the lemon loaf into 6, with 12 fruit buns)
Preparation time 15 minutes
Cooking time 20-35 minutes

Basic Cake Mix
6 eggs
350g (12oz) self-raising flour
350g (12oz) caster sugar
350g (12oz) soft butter
3 level teaspoons baking powder

Preheat the oven to 180°C/
Fan 160°C/Gas 4 for all cakes.

1 Measure all the ingredients into a large mixing bowl and beat until smooth.

Chocolate Cake with Wicked Chocolate Ganache Icing

Use half the basic cake mix above, plus the following.

TO ADD TO THE MIXTURE
40g (1 ½oz) cocoa powder
4 tablespoons boiling water

FOR SPREADING AND ICING
150 ml (¼ pint) double cream
150g (5oz) Bournville plain
    chocolate, broken into pieces
4 tablespoons apricot jam

1 Put the cocoa in a mixing bowl, and add the water slowly to make a stiff paste. Add to the half cake mixture.

2 Turn into two lined 18cm (7in) deep sandwich tins, level the top and bake in the preheated oven for about 20-25 minutes until shrinking away from the sides of the tin and springy to the touch.

3 Leave to cool in the tin, then turn on to a cooling rack to become completely cold before icing.

4 To make the icing, measure the cream and chocolate pieces into a bowl and carefully melt over a pan of hot water over a low heat, or gently in the

Cakes, top layer left to right: Almond Fruity Buns, Chocolate Cake, Lemon Drizzle Loaf

microwave. Stir until melted, then set aside to cool a little and to thicken up.

5 To ice the cake, spread the apricot jam on the top of each cake. Spread half of the ganache icing on to the top of one of the cakes, then sandwich the two cakes together. Use the remaining ganache icing to ice the top of the double cake in a swirl pattern. Dust with icing sugar to serve.

Lemon Drizzle Loaf Cake

Use half of the remaining basic cake mix above (a quarter of the original), plus the following.

the finely grated zest of ½ lemon

LEMON CRUNCHY ICING
50g (2oz) granulated sugar
juice of ½ lemon

1 Add the lemon zest to the basic cake mix, and turn into a lined 450g (1lb) loaf tin.

2 Bake in the preheated oven for about 35 minutes until golden brown, shrinking away from the sides of the tin and springy to the touch.

3 While the cake is still warm, make the topping. Mix together the sugar and lemon juice and pour over the warm cake.

4 Loosen the sides of the cake, then lift the cake out of the tin.

Almond Fruity Buns

Use the remaining quarter of the basic cake mix above, plus the following.

50g (2oz) sultanas
50g (2oz) dried apricots, snipped into small pieces
25g (1 oz) ground almonds

TOPPING
a few flaked almonds

1 Add the sultanas, apricots and ground almonds to the cake mixture, and stir until well mixed.

2 Turn into a 12-hole bun tin, lined with paper cases, and sprinkle with flaked almonds.

3 Bake in the preheated oven for about 20 minutes until golden brown and springy to the touch.

GOOD THINGS TO KNOW Modern baking powders are slower to react once the mix is made and put in the tin, so don't worry if it is an hour or so before you bake the cakes.

PREPARING AHEAD The chocolate cake will last three days in the fridge, but the icing will lose its shine. The lemon loaf and buns will last for three days as well. All will freeze well, but un-iced.

AGA

2-oven Aga Cook these one after the other, starting with the buns, then the chocolate cake and then the loaf, on grid shelf or floor of the roasting oven with the cold shelf on the second set of runners. The buns will take about 15-20 minutes, the chocolate cake about 20 minutes, the drizzle loaf about 30 minutes.

4-oven Aga Cook on the grid shelf on the floor of the baking oven without the cold shelf for about the same timings as above.

Lighter Simnel Cake (V)

This has become the traditional Easter cake, but originally it was given by servant girls to their mothers when they went home on Mothering Sunday. I think it's good at any time of year, not just Easter. This is not a deep cake, and has a layer of marzipan in the centre of the cake.

SERVES ABOUT 8-10
Preparation time 15 minutes
Cooking time about 1½-2 hours

175g (6oz) light muscovado sugar
175g (6oz) butter, softened
175g (6oz) self-raising flour
3 eggs
25g (1oz) ground almonds
2 tablespoons milk
100g (4oz) sultanas
100g (4oz) glacé cherries,
    quartered, washed and dried
100g (4oz) dried apricots, snipped
    into small pieces
100g (4oz) stem ginger, drained
    and finely chopped
1 teaspoon ground mixed spice
2 teaspoons ground ginger

FILLING AND TOPPING
450g (1lb) golden marzipan
3 tablespoons apricot jam
1 egg, beaten

Preheat the oven to 160°C/
Fan 140°C/Gas 3, and grease
and line the base and sides of
a 20cm (8in) deep round cake tin
with Bakewell paper.

PREPARING AHEAD *Make the cake ahead and freeze or, if your kitchen is cool, make ahead and store in an airtight cake tin for a month.*

1 Measure all the cake ingredients into a large mixing bowl and beat well until thoroughly blended. Place half the mixture into the prepared tin and level the surface.

2 Take one-third of the marzipan and roll out into a circle the same size as the cake tin. Place the circle on top of the cake mixture. Spoon the remaining cake mixture on top of the marzipan and level the surface.

3 Bake the cake in the preheated oven for about 1½-2 hours or until golden brown and firm on top. If towards the end of the cooking time the cake is getting too brown, loosely cover with a piece of foil. Allow the cake to cool in the tin before turning on to a cooling rack.

4 When the cake is cool, brush the top with a little warmed apricot jam. Roll out half the remaining marzipan to a circle the size of the cake and sit it on top. Crimp the edges of the marzipan and make a lattice pattern in the centre of the marzipan using a sharp knife. Make 11 even-sized balls from the remaining marzipan and arrange around the edge.

5 Brush the marzipan with beaten egg and glaze under a hot grill for about 5 minutes (turning the cake round so it browns evenly) so the marzipan is tinged brown all over. (You can also do this with a blow-torch if preferred.) Decorate with crystallised flowers if you like (see below).

GOOD THINGS TO KNOW *To crystallise primroses, narcissi or violets, arrange the fresh flowers on a cooling rack. Lightly whisk some egg white in a bowl, then carefully brush over the flower petals. Sprinkle over caster sugar so the sugar sticks to the egg white.*

Leave to harden, in a warm place, e.g. a shelf above a radiator or in an airing cupboard, until dry and firm. Carefully remove from the rack and arrange in the centre of the cake.

AGA

2-oven Aga Bake on the grid shelf on the floor of the roasting oven, with the cold sheet on the second set of runners for about 30-40 minutes until a perfect golden brown. Watch carefully. Transfer the hot cold sheet to the centre of the simmering oven and sit the cake on top. Continue to bake for a further 1-1 ½ hours until a skewer inserted comes out clean.

4-oven Aga Bake on the grid shelf on the floor of the baking oven for about 30-40 minutes, then transfer to the simmering oven for a further 1-1 ½ hours. To glaze the cake, wrap it round the sides in a double thickness of foil and sit in the roasting tin. Slide on to the top set of runners in the roasting oven for about 3 minutes to lightly brown the marzipan – watch like a hawk so it doesn't burn.

Chocolate Brownies with Swirled Topping (V)

These brownies are really moist because of the ground almonds. Don't be put off by the goat's cheese in the topping. We tested this recipe using mascarpone and Philadelphia, and the results were not nearly so good.

MAKES ABOUT 16 SQUARES
Preparation time 8 minutes
Cooking time 25-30 minutes

100g (4 oz) butter, cut into small
   cubes, plus extra for greasing
225g (8oz) Bournville plain
   chocolate, broken into small
   pieces
100g (4 oz) caster sugar
3 eggs, beaten
75g (3 oz) self-raising flour
75g (3 oz) ground almonds
1 teaspoon baking powder

TOPPING

150g (5oz) soft milk goat's cheese,
   e.g. a tub of Chavroux
75g (3 oz) caster sugar
½ teaspoon vanilla extract
1 egg, beaten

Preheat the oven to 180°C/
Fan 160°C/Gas 4. Line a traybake
tin of about 23 x 30cm (9 x 12in)
with foil, and butter it generously.

*PREPARING AHEAD You can
make the brownies two days
ahead, but they must be well
wrapped otherwise they will
dry out.*

1. Measure the butter and chocolate into a bowl and place over gently simmering water until just melted. When melted add the sugar, stir to combine and set aside to cool slightly.

2. Add the eggs gradually to the melted chocolate, beating after each addition. Fold in the flour, ground almonds and baking powder, and pour into the prepared tin.

3. Combine the topping ingredients and mix until smooth. Pour on to the chocolate mixture in the tin, spreading it evenly. Using a small palette knife, swirl the cheese into the chocolate to create a marbled effect.

4. Bake in the preheated oven for about 25-30 minutes until the mixture is just set.

5. Allow to cool before cutting into about 16 squares.

GOOD THINGS TO KNOW *If you don't like the idea of the goat's cheese topping, you can omit it, and just cook the brownies as they are.*

AGA

2-oven Aga Bake on the grid shelf on the floor of the roasting oven with the cold shelf on the second set of runners for about 25 minutes until the mixture is just set. Turn halfway through the cooking time.

4-oven Aga Bake on the grid shelf on the floor of the baking oven for about 25 minutes until the mixture is just set. Turn halfway through the cooking time. If it is getting too brown slide the cold shelf on the second set of runners above.

Tiny Lemon Drizzle Cakes (V)

Utterly delicious. If time is short, use bought sweet or shortcrust pastry. These are extra special when served warm: just heat for 20 seconds on full power in the microwave, a little longer if heating several at a time. This amount of pastry and filling makes enough to fill two 12-hole mini muffin tins.

MAKES 24 SMALL TARTS
Preparation time 15 minutes
Cooking time 15-20 minutes

SWEETCRUST PASTRY
175g (6oz) plain flour
75g (3oz) butter, cut into small
    cubes
25g (1oz) icing sugar
1 egg, beaten

FILLING AND TOPPING
about 4 tablespoons real lemon
    curd
juice of ½ lemon
50g (2oz) caster sugar

SPONGE
1 egg
50g (2oz) butter, softened
50g (2oz) caster sugar
50g (2oz) self-raising flour
finely grated zest of ½ lemon

Preheat the oven to 190°C/
Fan 170°C/Gas 5.

PREPARING AHEAD *These freeze very well cooked and un-iced. Defrost and ice on the day, or the day before serving.*

1 To make the pastry, measure the flour, butter and icing sugar into a processor and whiz together for a few moments until the mixture looks like breadcrumbs. Add the egg and continue to whiz until the pastry forms a dough. Wrap in clingfilm and chill in the fridge if time allows. If preferred rub the butter into the flour by hand, then mix in the beaten egg.

2 Roll the pastry out thinly on a lightly floured work surface. Using a small cutter cut out 24 rounds of pastry. Put each round on top of the muffin holes. Using your fingers, gently push each round of pastry into the holes. Spoon a ½ teaspoon lemon curd into the base of each case.

3 Measure the sponge ingredients into the unwashed processor and whiz together for a few seconds until smooth. Divide the sponge mixture between the pastry cases.

4 Slide the tins into the centre of the preheated oven and bake for about 15-20 minutes or until the sponge is well risen and golden brown on top and the pastry is cooked pale brown.

5 Whilst the tarts are baking, mix the lemon juice and caster sugar for the topping together in a small bowl. Lift the tarts out of the tin gently with a small palette knife. Pour the icing over the warm tarts and leave to cool on a wire rack.

GOOD THINGS TO KNOW *This same quantity will make larger tarts using one 12-hole muffin tin.*

AGA Slide the tin directly on to the floor of the roasting oven and bake for about 12-15 minutes until golden brown and the pastry is cooked.

Mincemeat and Cranberry Christmas Cake

I am often asked for my mincemeat cake recipe, which I did in one of my first books. This is a variation, what you might call a quick Christmas cake on the lighter side. This cake is shallow, but if you want a deeper one, cook in a 20cm (8in) round tin.

SERVES 8

Preparation time 10 minutes
Cooking time about 3-3 ½ hours

250g (9oz) self-raising flour
3 eggs
175g (6oz) butter, softened
175g (6oz) light muscovado sugar
175g (6oz) sultanas
175g (6oz) raisins
175g (6oz) currants
300g (10 oz) good mincemeat
50g (2oz) dried cranberries

TOPPING

4 tablespoons apricot jam
50g (2oz) dried cranberries
250g (9oz) white marzipan
icing sugar

Preheat the oven to 150°C/Fan 130°C/Gas 2, and grease and line a 23cm (9in) round cake tin.

PREPARING AHEAD *This cake can be made up to a month ahead, kept wrapped in foil in the fridge or cool larder. The icing will only last about a week, so store un-iced.*

1 Measure all the ingredients into a large mixing bowl and beat together using a wooden spoon or an electric hand whisk.

2 Spoon the mixture into the prepared cake tin and smooth the surface. Bake in the preheated oven for about 3-3 ½ hours, or until a skewer comes out clean when inserted in the middle. You may need to cover with foil if the top is getting too brown.

3 To make the topping, melt the apricot jam and use half to glaze over the top of the cake.

4 Knead the cranberries (keep about 10 for garnish) with the marzipan and roll out to slightly bigger than the top diameter of the cake. Lift on to the top of the cake and press down. Crimp around the edge. Glaze with the remaining apricot jam, if liked. Pile the reserved cranberries into the centre of the cake, garnish with a sprig of holly, and lightly dust with icing sugar.

GOOD THINGS TO KNOW *Dried cranberries can be found in good supermarkets or delis – in the dried fruit section or with the nuts at Christmas time.*

AGA

2-oven Aga Slide the cake on to the grid shelf on the floor of the roasting oven with the cold sheet on the second set of runners for about 40-45 minutes, until the cake is dark golden brown, turning carefully from time to time. Transfer to the simmering oven for about 1 hour 50 minutes-2 hours or until a skewer inserted into the centre of the cake comes out clean. You may have to cover the cake loosely with foil whilst in the simmering oven if getting too brown. Set aside to cool.

4-oven Aga Slide on to the grid shelf on the floor of the baking oven (without the cold sheet) for about 45 minutes, watching carefully, then transfer to the simmering oven when golden brown and cook as above.

Apple and Sultana Traybake (V)

A deliciously unusual traybake. Sometimes the cake dips a bit in the middle due to the apple softening, but don't worry, it tastes just as good!

MAKES ABOUT 21 SLICES
Preparation time 10 minutes
Cooking time 35-40 minutes

300g (10oz) dessert apples
juice of ½ lemon
350g (12oz) self-raising flour
2 slightly rounded teaspoons
    baking powder
350g (12oz) caster sugar
150g (5oz) sultanas
4 eggs
225g (8oz) butter, melted
1 teaspoon almond extract

ICING AND TOPPING
150ml (¼ pint) double cream,
    lightly whipped
about ½ x 450g jar good lemon
    curd
50g (2oz) flaked almonds

Preheat the oven to 180°C/
Fan 160°C/Gas 4. Line a traybake
tin or roasting tin of about 30 x
23cm (12 x 9in) with foil and
grease well.

1 Peel, core and thinly slice the apples and toss in the lemon juice.

2 Measure all the cake ingredients, except the apples, into a large bowl and mix well using an electric hand whisk.

3 Spread half the mixture into the prepared tin and arrange the apple slices on top in an even layer. Spoon the remaining mixture on top of the apples and level the top.

4 Bake in the preheated oven for about 35-40 minutes until golden brown and well risen. Set aside to cool.

5 Mix the cream and lemon curd for the icing together and spread over the cold cake. Sprinkle over the flaked almonds.

GOOD THINGS TO KNOW *The cake needs to be cold before the cream topping goes on, because the cream would run off a hot cake! When this traybake is just baked, it is delicious served as a warm pudding (without the topping), with cream or custard. It is best eaten fresh, whether warm or cold.*

AGA

2-oven Aga Bake on the grid shelf on the floor of the roasting oven with the cold sheet on the second set of runners for about 35 minutes or until just set, golden brown and well risen. Transfer the hot cold sheet to the simmering oven and bake for a further 30 minutes or until the cake is firm to the touch and shrinking away from the edges of the tin.

4-oven Aga Bake on the grid shelf on the floor of the baking oven for about 45 minutes, with the cold shelf on the second set of runners if getting too brown.

CHAPTER 7
DESSERTS AND PUDDINGS

There is a huge variety of desserts and puddings in this chapter, some cold and some hot, many of them fast to prepare and cook, with elements that can be prepared ahead. A number of them make use of helpful ingredients from the store-cupboard, and ready-made ingredients you can buy. One of the themes of this book is utilising bought items, and I am all in favour of many of these nowadays, as they have so improved in quality. Some of the best bought vanilla custards with added cream, for instance, are delicious, and save so much time; the same goes for ready-made pancakes and sponges for trifles. When you have things like this on the shelf, a pudding is easy and quick to prepare. I've even made a caramel mousse here, using Mars Bars!

Lots of the recipes here are very self-indulgent, but offer them in small pots or small slices. Because they have pots of flavour, no one will feel they have been deprived. But if you want to go for the simplicity of fresh things, offer fruit. I now go for a huge platter of thinly sliced fruits, which I put in the middle of the table. I think this looks more interesting than the traditional chopped fruit salad in a bowl, and it's a little simpler and quicker to do. You can bring out your artistic side, making your own picture on the plate. If you are really pushed for time, simply buy ready-prepared fruit salad and three-quarters fill smallish wine glasses with it, then add a couple of spoonfuls of Greek yoghurt and top with muscovado sugar. In half an hour the sugar will have melted, and the dessert is oh, so delicious!

There are some very glamorous puddings here, prime among them the hot passion soufflé and the white chocolate cheesecake. The Italian pannacotta is very popular at the moment, and my version, made with orange rind, is wonderful. It goes with many other puddings, as well as fresh fruit. There are a number of classics here, to which I have given a new twist.

I've also given a variety of sauces, which will go with bought ice-cream very nicely. Put scoops of ice-cream on a tray in the freezer, then when ready to serve, put a couple of scoops on each plate, top with some sauce, and you have a quick dessert everyone will enjoy.

Orange Pannacotta

Literally translated, 'pannacotta' means 'cooked cream'. It should be barely set, and it is delicious served with a sharp fruit or fruity coulis. If you prefer to make vanilla-flavoured ones, replace the orange rind with 1 teaspoon vanilla extract. As an alternative, the pannacotta may be set and served in pretty individual glasses and decorated with orange zest. A good accompaniment to an orange pannacotta is a sliced orange fruit salad.

SERVES 8
Preparation time 10 minutes, plus setting time

2 tablespoons cold water
1 x 11g packet powdered gelatine
900ml (1 ½ pints) single cream
75g (3oz) caster sugar
finely grated rind of 1 orange

You will need a 1.2 litre (2 pint) glass serving dish.

PREPARING AHEAD *The pannacotta can be made up to two days ahead, if kept in the fridge.*

1 Measure the cold water into a small container and sprinkle the gelatine over evenly. Set aside to sponge.

2 Put the cream, sugar and orange rind into a saucepan and bring to scalding point (just below boiling), stirring to dissolve the sugar. Remove from the heat, and cool very slightly.

3 Add the sponged gelatine and whisk until dissolved and smooth. Pour into the glass dish and when cold, cover with clingfilm and allow to set in the fridge for about 6 hours or, ideally, overnight. If you prefer not to eat the orange rind, strain first.

GOOD THINGS TO KNOW *If you prefer, you can use leaf gelatine (see page 188, Sea Breeze Jelly) or vegetarian gelatine which is based on seaweed, the setting agent being agar-agar.*

AND ANOTHER THING *To make individual moulds to turn out, use eight small metal pudding basins. Lightly oil the insides, and leave upside down on kitchen paper to allow excess oil to drain out. Make as above. Just before serving, gently using your index finger, pull the pannacotta from the side of the mould, turn out and serve with your chosen fruit.*

Each pannacotta is garnished with zest taken from a thin-skinned orange with a zester

Caribbean Banana Dessert

A very quick hot dessert, using some characteristic West Indian ingredients, which is absolutely delicious.

SERVES 4

Preparation time 5 minutes
Cooking time 5 minutes

4 bananas, slightly under-ripe
15g (½ oz) butter
50g (2oz) light muscovado sugar
2 tablespoons dark rum
4 tablespoons pouring double
  cream
45g (1 ½oz) ratafia biscuits or
  macaroons, coarsely crushed
icing sugar

1 Peel the bananas and cut in half lengthways. Slice the bananas into long thin slices.

2 Melt the butter in a large non-stick frying pan. Add the bananas and fry over a medium heat for about 30 seconds.

3 Sprinkle in the sugar, then pour in the rum and double cream.

4 Turn the bananas over in the sauce and swirl the pan around so the sauce becomes toffee-like.

5 Pour into a serving dish and sprinkle over the crushed biscuits.

6 Serve hot, dusted with icing sugar, with extra pouring cream.

GOOD THINGS TO KNOW *The bananas want to be still quite firm, as if they are too ripe when heated, they will just break apart.*

Wonderful White Chocolate Cheesecake

Serve very thin slices as this cheesecake is very rich, but so delicious!

SERVES 8 AT LEAST
Preparation time 20 minutes
Cooking time 45 minutes

BASE

50g (2oz) butter
150g (5oz) plain chocolate
  digestive biscuits, crushed

FILLING

300g (10oz) good-quality white
  chocolate
400g (14oz) full-fat cream cheese
2 eggs
150ml (¼ pint) soured cream
1 teaspoon vanilla extract

TO SERVE

a dusting of cocoa powder
about 225g (8oz) fresh strawberries
  or raspberries

Preheat the oven to 160°C/
Fan 140°C/Gas 3. Grease and
line the base of a 20cm (8in)
deep spring-form cake tin with
non-stick paper.

PREPARING AHEAD *You can
make this the night before.*

1 Melt the butter in a small saucepan over a low heat. Stir in the crushed biscuits and press evenly over the base of the prepared tin. Chill in the fridge.

2 Break the white chocolate into a bowl and melt over a pan of hot water (do not allow the chocolate to become too hot), stirring occasionally with a spoon until runny and smooth.

3 Whisk the cream cheese and eggs together in a large bowl until smooth, then add the soured cream and vanilla and whisk again until completely smooth with no lumps. Stir in the melted chocolate and mix together.

4 Pour this mixture into the tin and spread evenly over the chilled base. Bake in the preheated oven for about 45 minutes until firm around the edge and just set in the middle. Remove from the oven. Run a small palette knife around the edge of the tin, and then allow to cool and chill.

5 Remove the outside ring and lift the base on to a serving plate. Serve dusted with cocoa powder and with a few fresh strawberries or raspberries.

GOOD THINGS TO KNOW *White chocolate can be tricky to use when melted, so do not allow it to get too hot otherwise it becomes grainy. Milky Bar does not melt well – we prefer to use Lindt Continental White chocolate or Green and Black's.*

AND ANOTHER THING *The surface of the baked cheesecake may crack slightly in the middle, but don't*

worry, this is part of its charm! To avoid a really deep crack, loosen the tin around the edge before the cheesecake becomes cold.

AGA Pour into the tin and spread evenly over the chilled base. Bake on the grid shelf on the floor of the roasting oven with the cold sheet on the second set of runners for about 15 minutes until beginning to set around the edges.

Transfer the hot cold sheet to the simmering oven, sit the cheesecake on top and bake for about another 30 minutes until firm around the edge and just set in the middle. Remove from the oven. Using a small palette knife run the knife around the edge of the tin and then allow to cool and chill. Remove the outside ring and lift the base on to a serving plate.

Vodka Trifle with Cherries and Oranges

This trifle is very colourful as well as delicious. It is best made the day before, so that the flavours have time to develop. Serve cold. Trifle sponges come in packets of eight: you'll find them in the supermarket, usually in the custards and jelly section.

SERVES 6-8
Preparation time 15 minutes

1 x 250g tub mascarpone cheese
2 tablespoons vodka
finely grated zest of 2 oranges
300ml (½ pint) double cream, lightly whisked
12-16 trifle sponges
1 x 390g jar Bonne Maman cherry compote
3 oranges, peeled and segmented
8 Cape gooseberries to decorate
icing sugar

PREPARING AHEAD *This must be made a day in advance.*

1 Measure the mascarpone cheese, vodka and half the orange zest into a mixing bowl. Add the cream a little at a time to the cheese, beating well until smooth.

2 Split the trifle sponges horizontally.

3 Spread half of the cheese mixture across the bottom of a round 26cm (10 ½in) shallow glass dish. Arrange half of the split sponges on the cheese mixture and press down gently. (The number of sponges you use will vary with the size of the dish you have.) Spoon the cherry compote on top, spreading right to the edges of the bowl. Arrange the orange segments on top and the remaining trifle sponges on the fruit. Spread the remaining cheese mixture over the surface.

4 Scatter the reserved orange zest over the trifle, cover with clingfilm and leave in the fridge for the sponges to soak, ideally overnight.

5 The next day, arrange the Cape gooseberries around the edge. Dust with a little icing sugar just before serving.

GOOD THINGS TO KNOW *Cape gooseberries are also called physalis and Chinese lanterns. They are small golden berries with a thin papery husk which for decoration is folded back to expose the berry, and looks most attractive and delicious to eat.*

Iced Bramble Flummery

Brambles and blackberries are the same fruit. They are great to have in the freezer as a standby pudding, especially in the summer. The brambles are not cooked so the flavour is very fresh.

SERVES 8-12

Preparation time 10 minutes, plus freezing time

450g (1lb) fresh or frozen blackberries
300ml (½ pint) double cream
juice of 1 large lemon
600ml (1 pint) milk
100g (4oz) caster sugar
a few fresh blackberries and mint to garnish

You will need a 1.5 litre (2 ¾ pint) plastic container, and 8-12 ramekins.

1 Put the blackberries into a processor, and whiz until smooth. Sieve, saving the juice, and discard the pips.

2 Whisk the cream using an electric hand whisk until you have soft peaks. Stir in the fruit purée, lemon juice, milk and sugar and mix well. Pour into the plastic container, cover and freeze overnight or for a minimum of 12 hours.

3 Remove from the freezer, and thaw just enough so that it cuts into large chunks with a knife. Whiz again in the processor until smooth and a thick pouring consistency.

4 Pour into individual ramekins, sit on a tray and cover with clingfilm. Freeze until set or needed.

5 To serve, remove the ramekins from the freezer about 15 minutes before serving so that they soften a bit (on a really hot day, just put in the fridge for 15 minutes). Decorate each ramekin with a few blackberries and a sprig of fresh mint.

GOOD THINGS TO KNOW *Frozen blackberries are far cheaper than raspberries and they make a delicious coulis too (see the Fast Sauces on page 198). If you have an abundance of raspberries in the summer, of course, you can use them instead of blackberries.*

Sea Breeze Jelly with Pink Grapefruit

A very light and impressive pudding, perfect for that special occasion – and great novelty value too! Serve it in cocktail glasses.

SERVES 6
Preparation time 5 minutes

1 pink grapefruit
3 good tablespoons vodka –
   or more if you like!
cranberry juice from a carton
1 x 11g packet powdered gelatine
25g (1oz) caster sugar

TO DECORATE
thin slices of lime and fresh or
   dried cranberries

PREPARING AHEAD *You can make the jellies a day in advance, but bring them to room temperature before serving.*

1 Segment the grapefruit over a measuring jug to catch any juice. Measure the vodka into the measuring jug with the juice and make up to 600ml (1 pint) with cranberry juice.

2 Measure 2 tablespoons of the cranberry liquid into a small bowl and sprinkle the gelatine evenly over it. Set aside to sponge.

3 Put the sugar into a saucepan, add half the juice and heat gently until just below boiling point.

4 Tip the sponged gelatine out of the bowl into the hot juice, and stir briskly until melted. Add the remaining cranberry liquid.

5 Put 2 grapefruit segments into each cocktail glass and pour on the fruit juice. Transfer to the fridge and allow to set.

6 To serve, garnish each glass with a thin slice of lime and a cranberry on a cocktail stick!

GOOD THINGS TO KNOW
1 x 11g packet of powdered gelatine sets 600ml (1 pint) of liquid. If you prefer to use leaf gelatine, use 4 leaves instead. Soak the leaves in cold water until pliable, about a minute, then add to hot liquid to dissolve.

Ebony and Ivory Chocolate Pots

These look stunning made in small glasses, but of course you can make them in small ramekins or coffee cups if preferred. They are very rich, so make them very small.

SERVES 6

Preparation time 15 minutes

150g (5oz) white chocolate (Lindt)
1 x 400ml tub half-fat crème fraîche
150g (5oz) dark chocolate (Bournville)
about 6 large strawberries, sliced into quarters

PREPARING AHEAD *Make the day before.*

1 Break the white chocolate into a heatproof bowl and pour over 200ml (7fl oz) of the crème fraîche.

2 Sit the bowl over a saucepan of simmering water and melt over a low heat until smooth, stirring occasionally (make sure you do not get the chocolate too hot otherwise it will go grainy). Pour into a jug.

3 In a clean bowl do exactly the same as above with the dark chocolate and remaining crème fraîche. Melt until smooth. Pour into another jug.

4 Arrange six small glasses in front of you and with a jug in each hand pour both chocolates into each glass at the same time. This means that you get a different coloured chocolate each side of the glass with a ripple effect in the middle. Leave a gap at the top of the glass for the strawberries.

5 Transfer to the fridge to set for a minimum of an hour.

6 To serve, remove from the fridge for about 2 hours, and arrange the strawberry quarters on top of the set mixture.

GOOD THINGS TO KNOW *You can melt dark chocolate in the microwave with or without cream. Simply put the chocolate and cream in a bowl – no need to cover. Melt in short blasts on half power, stirring as you check it. Don't overheat, just allow it to melt. White chocolate can be tricky to melt, so it is advisable to do this in the traditional way over simmering water.*

Apricot and Brandy Fool

Such a quick and simple pudding, which is good eaten by itself, but it is delicious with canned peaches too.

SERVES 6

Preparation time 10 minutes

2 x 400g cans apricots, drained
1 tablespoon brandy
150ml (¼ pint) pouring double cream
300ml (½ pint) fresh custard from a carton
2 tablespoons icing sugar, sieved
juice of ½ lemon

1 Thinly slice 6 apricots and arrange them in the base of six stemmed glasses or ramekins. Pour over a little brandy.

2 Put the remaining apricots in a food processor and whiz until a purée, with no lumps.

3 Lightly whip the double cream with a whisk, then fold in the apricot purée. Stir in the custard, icing sugar and lemon juice.

4 Spoon the mixture into the glasses and chill in the fridge for a minimum of an hour.

GOOD THINGS TO KNOW *If you like more of a creamy texture to the fool, use thick double cream and then there is no need to whip it.*

Fresh Fruit Salad Platter

A perfect end to a meal, to serve either on its own, or as an alternative choice to a rich dessert. Buy whatever you find in the market, using seasonal fruit, and arrange them to look attractive.

SERVES 4-6
Preparation time 10 minutes

1 small ripe cantaloupe melon
1 ripe mango
450g (1lb) cherries
225g (8oz) ripe strawberries, hulled
4 fresh figs, halved
fresh mint to garnish

1 Slice the melon in half. Scoop out the seeds and remove the skin. Cut into fairly thin wedges.

2 To prepare the mango, cut either side of the flat stone, and remove the skin with a knife. Slice the mango thinly.

3 Divide the sliced melon into two piles. Take a large round platter and fan the melon out, half on one side of the plate and the other half opposite.

4 Divide the sliced mango into two piles. Arrange these in between the melon, leaving a gap on either side. (You should have a round plate like a clockface with melon at 12 and 6 o'clock and mango at 3 and 9 o'clock!)

5 Divide the cherries into two piles. Arrange them in between the melon and mango on both sides of the plate. Arrange the strawberries in the remaining gaps.

6 Arrange the halved figs around the plate, and garnish with fresh mint.

GOOD THINGS TO KNOW *Vary the fruits with the seasons, but avoid those that discolour when cut (such as apples, pears and peaches).*

Cheat's Caramel Mousse

So fast to make, but your guests will think you've been creating for hours! In fact you could have done them hours before, as they need to be well chilled and set. You can also make this recipe using Snickers Bars instead of Mars Bars.

SERVES 4

Preparation time 10 minutes, plus setting time

1 tablespoon milk
3 x 62.5g Mars Bars, thinly sliced
300ml (½ pint) double cream, lightly whipped

DECORATION

4 tablespoons double cream, whipped
8 Maltesers

1 Put the milk and Mars Bars slices in a heatproof bowl. Melt over hot water or in the microwave for about 3-4 minutes, stirring halfway through, until smooth and completely melted. Set aside to cool a little.

2 Fold the whipped cream into the caramel mixture and spoon into four size 1 ramekins or glasses. Transfer to the fridge to set for about an hour for a soft set, or overnight for a firmer set.

3 Decorate just before serving with a blob of whipped cream topped with Maltesers, halved or whole.

GOOD THINGS TO KNOW *When heating chocolate over hot water be careful not to get the water too hot otherwise the chocolate will go lumpy. Remember chocolate melts in a child's pocket on a warm day – so very little heat is needed.*

Tiramisù Revisited

A wonderful Italian trifle, which is really quick, and it doesn't use raw eggs. 'Tiramisù' actually means 'pick me up' in Italian!

SERVES 6-8
Preparation time 10 minutes

1 generous teaspoon instant coffee
100ml (4fl oz) boiling water
90ml (3fl oz) brandy
25g (1oz) caster sugar
1 x 250g tub mascarpone cheese
1 x 500g tub or carton of good-quality custard
1 packet trifle sponges, containing 8 sponges
75g (3oz) plain chocolate, coarsely grated or chopped

PREPARING AHEAD *Make a few hours ahead, or the day before. It won't come to any harm.*

1 Dissolve the coffee in the water, and mix with the brandy and sugar.

2 Whisk the mascarpone in a bowl with an electric hand whisk, then whisk in the custard.

3 Split the sponge cakes horizontally and line a fairly shallow glass dish, about 23cm (9in) round, with half of them. With a pastry brush, brush over half the coffee and brandy liquid. Spoon over half of the mascarpone mixture and sprinkle over half the chocolate. Arrange a second layer of sponge and soak with the remaining coffee and brandy liquid. Spoon over the remaining mascarpone mixture and sprinkle with the rest of the chocolate.

4 Chill for up to a few hours before serving.

GOOD THINGS TO KNOW *This will also make eight individual tiramisùs in small wine glasses. These take longer to assemble, but look good and are easy to serve as part of a buffet.*

Raspberry and Almond Trifle

If you haven't got any sherry or Framboise, you could use Kirsch or vodka. You can buy really good vanilla custard in cartons from the supermarket in varying quantities now, but be sure to buy the best you can.

SERVES 6-8
Preparation time 15 minutes

350g (12oz) frozen raspberries
100ml (4fl oz) medium dry sherry or
    Framboise (raspberry liqueur)
1 packet trifle sponges, containing
    8 sponges
raspberry jam
about 10 ratafia biscuits or
    macaroons, coarsely crushed
600ml (1pint) bought vanilla
    custard
150ml (¼ pint) double cream,
    whipped
a few flaked almonds, toasted

PREPARING AHEAD *Make a day ahead and serve chilled.*

1 Put the frozen raspberries in a bowl, pour the sherry over and leave to thaw.

2 Split the sponges in half, and sandwich together with raspberry jam. Arrange in the base of a shallow dish of about 20cm (8in) diameter, and 6cm (2 ½in) deep.

3 Spoon over the raspberries and sherry. Sprinkle over the crushed ratafia biscuits, and level gently with the back of a metal spoon.

4 Carefully pour over the custard.

5 Decorate with blobs of softly whipped cream and sprinkle with flaked almonds. Serve chilled.

GOOD THINGS TO KNOW *If you cannot buy toasted almonds, toast them yourself in a dry pan over a medium heat on the hob. The natural oil will come out of the almonds and they will brown, but don't take your eyes off them for a second as they can easily burn.*

Fast Dessert Sauces

Luxury Vanilla Custard Buy a tub of the best custard you can buy. Heat with a little extra double cream and vanilla extract, or simply add cream to the custard and serve cold without heating. Serves 4-6 with fruit, pies or crumbles.

Chocolate Ganache Sauce Melt together in a bowl 150g (5oz) plain chocolate, broken into pieces, and 150ml (¼ pint) double cream. Stand the bowl over a pan of hot, not simmering, water until melted, give a good stir and serve with ice-cream or meringues. Serves 4-6.

Toffee Sauce I can eat this toffee sauce straight out of the pan by itself – not too good for the waistline! Measure 150g (5oz) light muscovado sugar on the scale pan, then spread it out and spoon 150g (5oz) golden syrup on top to make a total weight of 300g (10oz). Tip into a saucepan, add 50g (2oz) butter, and mix together. Simmer for about 5 minutes, stirring all the time. Remove from the heat, add a 170g can evaporated milk, and stir well. It is now ready to serve hot or cold. Keeps in the fridge for a month, but I doubt it will last that long! Good with bananas, ice-cream and plain creamy puddings. Serves 8.

Raspberry Coulis Measure 500g (1lb 2oz) raspberries into a processor (these can be fresh or thawed frozen), add icing sugar to taste (about 75g/3oz) and whiz until smooth. Push the purée through a sieve to remove any pips, then store in the fridge for up to a week or freeze for up to a year. Serve with meringues and cream or fresh red fruits. Serves 6-8.

Rum and Raisin Sauce Measure 500g (1lb 2oz) caster sugar into a pan with 150ml (¼ pint) cold water. Gently heat until the sugar has dissolved and the liquid is clear. Boil for a minute. Remove from the heat, cool until warm and stir in 150ml (¼ pint) rum or brandy and 450g (1lb) raisins. Cool, then pour into two glass jars with screwtop lids. Use over the next three months. If the sugar crystallises, just heat, add a little more water, stir and cool. Perfect to have in the cupboard at the ready to pour over good ice-cream (vanilla or chocolate), or serve with Greek yoghurt. Serves about 8.

Glory Farm Crumble

Oh, so good, and so easy to make. This crumble is in the oven for about 40 minutes and will cook whilst you're having the main course. Use other fruits in season such as apples and raspberries, apricots or plums.

SERVES 6

Preparation time 10 minutes
Cooking time 40 minutes

750g (1 ¾lb) cooking apples, peeled, cored and chopped into 2.5cm (1in) pieces
225g (8oz) blackberries
50g (2oz) demerara sugar
3 tablespoons water

CRUMBLE TOPPING

225g (8oz) fruit muesli with added nuts
100g (4oz) butter, at room temperature
75g (3oz) demerara sugar

Preheat the oven to 200°C/
Fan 180°C/Gas 6.

PREPARING AHEAD *You could prepare the muesli topping in advance.*

1 Mix together the apples, blackberries, sugar and water in a bowl, and stir using your hands. Tip into a 1.5 litre (2¾ pint) deep ovenproof dish – I use a pie dish.

2 Measure the muesli and butter into a food processor and whiz for a few seconds until roughly chopped. Remove the blade, stir in the sugar and spread over the top of the fruit in the dish. Cover the dish loosely with foil.

3 Bake in the preheated oven for about 30-40 minutes, removing the foil for the last 10 minutes, until the fruit is cooked and the topping is crisp.

GOOD THINGS TO KNOW *If using frozen blackberries, omit the water from the ingredients as the base of the crumble will become too wet.*

AGA Slide on to the second set of runners in the roasting oven for about 35 minutes until the fruit is cooked and the topping is crisp.

Hot Passion Soufflés

Soufflés are always very impressive, and they're not nearly as difficult as you may think. Don't overcook them, though, as they want to be soft in the centre.

SERVES 6
Preparation time 10 minutes
Cooking time 10 minutes

butter for greasing
8 passionfruits
about 150ml (¼ pint) orange juice
   from a carton
1 rounded tablespoon cornflour
3 eggs, separated
100g (4oz) caster sugar
icing sugar

Preheat the oven to 200°C/
Fan 180°C/Gas 6. Generously
butter the inside of six size 1
ramekins.

PREPARING AHEAD *The soufflés can be made ahead until the end of step 5 and kept in the fridge for 6 hours. Then they can be cooked when needed, but being cold they will take a little longer in the oven.*

1 Cut the passionfruits in half, scoop out the pulp and sieve into a measuring jug. If time is short don't sieve out the pips. Make up to 225ml (8fl oz) with orange juice.

2 Slake the cornflour with 2 tablespoons of the fruit juice. Heat the remaining fruit juice, until boiling, and pour on to the cornflour mixture, stirring continually. Return to the pan, and bring to the boil to thicken.

3 Whisk the egg whites on full speed with an electric whisk until like a cloud. Gradually add the sugar a teaspoon at a time, still whisking on maximum speed, until it becomes stiff and glossy.

4 Beat the egg yolks into the thickened fruit juice. Mix in 2 generous tablespoons of meringue and finally fold in the remaining whisked egg whites.

5 Divide the mixture between the prepared ramekins and fill to the top. Level the surface and run the point of a teaspoon around the edge, pushing the mixture slightly inwards (this will allow it to rise evenly).

6 Gently transfer the ramekins to a small roasting tin, and pour in enough boiling water to come halfway up the sides of the ramekins.

7 Bake in the centre of the preheated oven for about 10 minutes until risen. Dust with icing sugar and serve at once. The centre should still be slightly soft.

GOOD THINGS TO KNOW *When a recipe calls for orange juice and it is heated, i.e. in a soufflé or sauce, use a good orange juice from a carton – the sort you have in the fridge for breakfast. If the recipe is not heated and therefore you would get the full fresh flavour use freshly squeezed oranges.*

AGA Bake on the grid shelf on the floor of the roasting oven for about 8 minutes.

Apple and Cinnamon Pancakes

These are bought pancakes, filled with a cinnamon and apple mixture – so quick to do, to make ahead and cook in one dish. You could use windfall apples or even apples that are past their best from the fruit bowl. If they are eating apples, the texture will be a little firmer.

SERVES 4

Preparation time 25 minutes
Cooking time 12 minutes

50g (2oz) butter, plus extra for
   greasing
2 large cooking apples, peeled
   and sliced
75g (3oz) demerara sugar, plus
   extra for sprinkling
½ teaspoon ground cinnamon
4 ready-made pancakes
about 40g (1½oz) butter, melted

Preheat the oven to 200°C/
Fan 180°C/Gas 6. Well butter a
shallow ovenproof dish, large
enough to take four rolled-up
pancakes.

PREPARING AHEAD *Keep the filled pancakes covered in the fridge until needed. The time in the oven will be longer, about 20 minutes.*

1 Melt the butter in a saucepan, add the apples, sugar and cinnamon, and stir over a high heat for a few minutes. Lower the heat and cook for about 15 minutes, uncovered, until the apples are soft.

2 Lie one pancake out on the work surface, spoon a quarter of the filling into the middle and roll to a cigar shape. Transfer to a buttered dish and continue with the remaining pancakes and apple.

3 Brush the pancakes with a little melted butter and sprinkle with a little extra demerara sugar.

4 Bake in the preheated oven for about 10-12 minutes or until piping hot in the middle.

5 Serve warm, with cream, crème fraîche or vanilla ice-cream.

GOOD THINGS TO KNOW *Ready-made pancakes are sold in all good supermarkets pre-packed like tortillas. They are very good, and perfect for a recipe like this, which is cooked again in the oven.*

AGA Slide on to the second set of runners in the roasting oven for about 10 minutes.

Lemon Soufflé Pudding

This pudding is at its best as soon as it comes out of the oven. The top is light and fluffy, and there is a lemon sauce underneath.

SERVES 4-6

Preparation time 10 minutes
Cooking time 30 minutes

50g (2oz) butter, softened, plus
    extra for greasing
100g (4oz) caster sugar
2 eggs, separated
50g (2oz) plain flour
300ml (½ pint) milk
finely grated zest and juice
    of 2 lemons

Preheat the oven to 180°C/
Fan 160°C/Gas 4. Lightly butter
a 1.2 litre (2 pint) shallow ovenproof
dish.

1 Measure the butter, sugar, egg yolks and flour together into a bowl, and whisk using an electric hand whisk until smooth. Slowly add the milk, then stir in the lemon zest and juice; expect it to curdle.

2 Whisk the egg whites until they form soft peaks, then carefully fold into the milk mixture.

3 Pour the mixture into the dish.

4 Slide into the preheated oven and bake for about 25-30 minutes or until golden brown on top and just set in the middle.

5 Serve at once with pouring cream.

GOOD THINGS TO KNOW *When stirring the egg whites into the milk mixture be careful not to knock any air out of them, as the topping mixture needs to be light and airy.*

AGA Stand the dish in a roasting tin and pour in boiling water to come half way up the dish. Bake on the grid shelf on the floor of the roasting oven for about 20 minutes. If getting too brown, slide the cold shelf above.

Ginger Spiced Pudding with Toffee Sauce

Delicious served cold as a cake without the toffee sauce, or warm as a pudding, as below.
I prefer it warm with the sauce, and like to serve slices of fresh mango with it too.

SERVES 6

Preparation time 10 minutes
Cooking time 35 minutes

50g (2oz) butter, melted, plus extra
    for greasing
100g (4oz) light muscovado sugar,
    plus extra for dusting
100g (4oz) plain flour
½ teaspoon bicarbonate of soda
2 teaspoons ground cinnamon
1 teaspoon ground ginger
¼ teaspoon freshly grated nutmeg
1 egg, beaten
75g (3oz) black treacle
125ml (4 ½fl oz) milk

TO SERVE

1 mango, cut into thin slices
Toffee Sauce (see page 198)

Preheat the oven to 180°C/
Fan 160°C/Gas 4. You will need
a 1kg (2 ¼lb) loaf tin, which you
should generously butter and dust
with light muscovado sugar.

1 Measure all the dry ingredients, except for the sugar, into a large bowl. In a separate bowl mix the egg, sugar, treacle, milk and melted butter together and beat until smooth and there are no lumps.

2 Stir the wet ingredients into the dry ingredients and beat hard for about a minute until smooth. Pour into the loaf tin (it will only part fill the tin).

3 Bake in the preheated oven for about 35 minutes until dark in colour, shrinking away from the sides of the tin and springy to the touch. Cover loosely with foil if getting too dark.

4 Arrange slices of mango on a plate and sit a slice of ginger pudding on top. Serve warm with warm toffee sauce.

GOOD THINGS TO KNOW *When we tested this recipe we also tried using self-raising flour and no bicarbonate of soda. It worked well but we preferred the sticky texture when old-fashioned bicarbonate of soda was used. Expect the loaf to be very shallow – when we cooked it in a 450g (1lb) loaf tin, it overflowed.*

AGA

2-oven Aga Put the small grill rack upside down in a small roasting tin. Sit the loaf tin on top and slide on to the grid shelf on the floor of the roasting oven with the cold shelf on the second set of runners for about 25-30 minutes.

4-oven Aga Cook as above in the baking oven, but without the cold shelf.

Apple and Almond Tart

This tart looks wonderful when it is cooked, as the pastry cover moulds itself to the shape of the apples. If you use an ovenproof china flan dish, rather than a tin, the tart will take longer to cook.

SERVES 8
Preparation time 20 minutes
Cooking time 25 minutes

PASTRY
300g (10oz) plain flour
150g (5oz) icing sugar
150g (5oz) butter, cubed
1 egg

FILLING AND TOPPING
175g (6oz) marzipan, coarsely grated
900g (2lb) dessert apples, peeled, cored and each sliced into 6-8 wedges
icing sugar

Preheat the oven to 220°C/ Fan 200°C/Gas 7. Preheat a baking sheet to get very hot.

You will need a 25cm (10in) fluted, loose-bottomed flan tin.

PREPARING AHEAD *You can cook the tart in advance and reheat it if you want.*

1 Measure the flour, icing sugar and butter into a processor. Whiz until it resembles a crumble. Add the egg and process until the mixture holds together. Gather together on a floured work surface. Wrap in clingfilm and rest in the fridge for about 15 minutes.

2 Take off a little less than half the chilled pastry for the top and return to the fridge. Roll out the rest of the pastry to make a circle large enough to line the flan tin. The pastry is a bit on the soft side, but patches up easily.

3 Spread the grated marzipan over the base of the flan then arrange the apple wedges on top of the marzipan. Roll out any pastry trimmings with the remaining pastry for the lid. Damp the edge of the rim of the pastry in the flan tin. Lift the pastry over the top of the fruit and press the two layers of pastry together, patching the edges if necessary.

4 Carefully, slide the tin directly on to the preheated baking sheet and bake in the preheated oven for about 20 minutes. Watch carefully as the edges will brown first. If the edges are getting too dark, cover the sides with a circle of foil.

5 Sieve some icing sugar over before serving. Serve hot with cream or crème fraîche.

GOOD THINGS TO KNOW *This is a good recipe for using up leftover marzipan from your Christmas cake.*

AGA Bake on the floor of the roasting oven with the cold plain shelf on the second set of runners for about 20 minutes, protecting the edges with foil if getting too brown.

Treacle Orange Sponge Puddings

These individual puddings are cooked in the oven in a roasting tin filled with water (bain-marie), which gives the same results as steaming in a pan but is easier. Using the whole of the orange, including the skin, gives the puddings a superb zesty flavour. They are nicest made on the day.

SERVES 8
Preparation time 15 minutes
Cooking time 1 ½ hours

175g (6 oz) butter, softened, plus
 extra for greasing
1 large thin-skinned orange
14 tablespoons golden syrup
3 eggs
175g (6oz) golden caster sugar
175g (6oz) self-raising flour
1 rounded teaspoon baking
 powder

Preheat the oven to 180ºC/Fan
160ºC/Gas 4. Butter eight 175ml
(6fl oz) metal pudding basins.

1 Cut eight very thin slices from the middle of the orange and reserve. Remove and discard the pips from the remaining orange pieces and process (including the skin) in a processor to a coarse, even texture.

2 Spoon 1 tablespoon of golden syrup into each pudding basin and top with a slice of orange, cutting a slit to the centre so that it sits flat in the base of the basin.

3 Measure the remaining ingredients, except the remaining golden syrup, into a large bowl with 3 tablespoons of the chopped orange pulp. Whisk together with an electric hand whisk until just blended. Divide between the basins.

4 Butter eight small squares of foil (large enough to cover the basins). Make a pleat in the centre of each piece of foil and cover the basins, buttered side down. Fold in the edges to seal tightly.

5 Place the basins in a large roasting tin and fill the tin with enough boiling water to come halfway up the side of the basins. Cover the roasting tin loosely with foil and bake for 1 ½ hours until the puddings are well risen and firm.

6 Leave to stand for about 5 minutes, then remove the foil and loosen the edges with a palette knife. Just before serving, gently heat the remaining 6 tablespoons of golden syrup with the remaining orange pulp for about 3 minutes to get hot.

7 Turn out the puddings and serve with the sauce poured over the top.

GOOD THINGS TO KNOW *Golden syrup slips easily off the spoon when the spoon is hot, so dip in boiling water for a few seconds before using.*

AND ANOTHER THING *To make one large pudding, use a 1.5 litre (2 ¾ pint) basin. Place the same amount of golden syrup as above, in the basin first and top with the 8 orange slices, overlapping them slightly. Cook in a large pan of simmering water for about 2-2¼ hours on the hob. For the AGA, bring a pan of water to the boil on the boiling plate, Add the pudding, then cover and simmer on the simmering plate for about 30 minutes. Transfer to the simmering oven for about 3 hours until cooked.*

AGA Slide the roasting tin on to the grid shelf on the floor of the roasting oven for about 25 minutes. Turn round once and continue to bake for a further 25 minutes until well risen and firm to the touch. Keep warm for up to 40 minutes in the roasting tin in the simmering oven, still covered with foil.

CHAPTER 8
DRINKS FOR ALL SEASONS

Home-produced drinks are very special, and I don't just mean an iced jug of diluted orange squash! Here you'll find some cooling drinks for summer, refreshing drinks for when you are hot or thirsty, drinks which can contribute to health, and some which are warming in the depths of winter. Most of them are non-alcoholic.

In the spring and summer it's nice to drink iced tea in the afternoon, and my husband enthusiastically vouches for the revivifying qualities of what he calls 'gunners' (please don't ask me where the name comes from, I just don't know!). My elderflower 'champagne' – so called, because it is deliciously fizzy when diluted – is an update on the elderflower cordial I have been making for years, and the lemon and lime fizz is something Lucy, Lucinda and I dreamed up after a long and warm afternoon's session at the Aga. Fruit smoothies are very fashionable at the moment, and although I suggest one

particular mixture, you could use anything you like, it's a matter of looking at the fruit bowl and seeing what is there, or using fruits in season. You could even use milk instead of the juice, or indeed some ice-cream. My grandchildren love them, and don't realise that they are getting a good dose of fruit goodness...

Of the three alcoholic drinks here, Bellini – that inspired Venetian marriage of champagne and peach juice – is the one I most associate with summer. The other two are warming winter treats. I have made my Christmas mulled wine for years, and it's ideal for a drinks party over the festive season. One of its major advantages is that it can be made ahead. If there is any left – which is unlikely – you can keep it in the fridge and have it on the next cold day. Irish coffee too, is a wonderfully warming autumn and winter drink, which I would offer to special guests at dinner. It makes a delicious end to a meal.

Mango and Banana Smoothie

Smoothies are very much the in-drink at the moment, and they can be enjoyed by all ages. They are healthy too, as there is no need to add sugar.

SERVES 6
(MAKES ABOUT 900ML/1 ½ PINTS)
Preparation time 5 minutes

1 very large mango
2 bananas
300ml (½ pint) orange juice
 from a carton
ice cubes, to serve

PREPARING AHEAD

This can be made a few hours ahead and kept in the fridge, but it is best made and drunk on the same day.

1 Cut the mango either side of the flat stone in the middle of the fruit. Peel the skin off, and roughly chop the flesh.

2 Peel and slice the bananas.

3 Put the mango and banana into a food processor and whiz until smooth.

4 Pour in the orange juice and whiz again until blended and there are no lumps.

5 Serve chilled with a couple of lumps of ice.

GOOD THINGS TO KNOW Smoothies are delicious made from any blends of soft or exotic fruits without pips. Try strawberry and banana, mango and paw-paw with a little added fresh lime juice. If you want, add yoghurt or single cream (this will make it richer) to any of the smoothies with banana. If adding milk only, you will have to add banana to get the right smoothie consistency.

Elderflower Champagne (Non-alcoholic)

This is my classic elderflower cordial recipe, but I have added Campden tablets, used in wine making, to give the cordial a longer life.

**MAKES ABOUT 1.5 LITRES
(2 ½ PINTS)**
Preparation time 15 minutes

1.6kg (3 ½lb) granulated sugar
1.4 litres (2 ½ pints) water
3 lemons
about 25 elderflower heads
50g (2oz) citric acid
2 Campden tablets
chilled fizzy water and ice cubes,
    to serve

PREPARING AHEAD *The champagne base will keep for a few months, but use up within six months.*

1 Measure the sugar and water into a large pan. Bring to the boil, stirring, until the sugar has dissolved. Remove from the heat and cool.

2 Slice the lemons thinly by hand or in a food processor. Put into a large plastic box or bucket.

3 Add the elderflower heads to the lemons with the citric acid and Campden tablets. Pour over the cooled sugar syrup. Cover and leave overnight or up to a couple of days.

4 Sieve and strain through muslin into bottles and store in the fridge (see below).

5 To serve, dilute to taste with chilled fizzy water and ice. If making in a jug, float some lemon or lime slices and fresh mint on the top.

GOOD THINGS TO KNOW *Elderflower heads can be picked from the hedgerows from the end of May for about a month. They can be frozen if liked; freeze in bags of 25 heads and remove straight from the freezer into the hot syrup. Do not defrost first, otherwise they turn the syrup a sludgy brown colour. Citric acid and Campden tablets can be bought from all good pharmacies.*

Real Irish Coffee

Delicious after a special meal or a long walk on a cold winter's day ... or think of your own excuse!

SERVES 2
Preparation time 10 minutes

4 teaspoons caster sugar
300ml (½ pint) good hot, strong
    black coffee
4 good tablespoons Irish whiskey
about 3 tablespoons pouring
    double cream, chilled

1 Warm a heatproof glass or small coffee cup with hot water. Pour out.

2 Add the sugar and a little of the hot coffee to each glass or cup, and stir to dissolve the sugar. Add the whiskey.

3 Pour in the remaining hot coffee, but not quite to the brim.

4 Gently pour the double cream on to the back of a teaspoon held over the coffee. The cream should float on the top.

GOOD THINGS TO KNOW *It is very important to use pouring double cream, as single cream or thick cream would sink to the bottom of the glass. The sugar also helps to prevent the cream sinking. The coffee can of course be served without cream if preferred.*

AND ANOTHER THING *For a change use Tia Maria or Grand Marnier instead of whiskey if preferred.*

Drinks, left to right: Lemon and Lime Fizz, Real Irish Coffee, Elderflower Champagne, Mango and Banana Smoothie

Christmas Mulled Wine

For an extra kick for a very special Christmas, add a glass of sherry or brandy just before serving.

MAKES 12 GLASSES, LESS IF THE GLASSES ARE LARGE
Preparation time 10 minutes
Cooking time 1 hour

4 lemons
2 large oranges
2 bottles red wine
1.2 litres (2 pints) water
16 cloves
2 cinnamon sticks
about 150g (5oz) caster sugar

1 Peel the zest very thinly from 3 lemons and 1 orange, and squeeze the juice. Thinly slice the remaining orange and lemon. Quarter the slices, put on a plate, cover and reserve for garnish.

2 Pour the wine, water, citrus peel and juices into a large pan, and add the cloves and cinnamon sticks. Bring to simmering point, cover and keep simmering for about an hour. Stir in sugar to taste.

3 Strain and serve hot with the reserved orange and lemon slices floating on top.

GOOD THINGS TO KNOW Can be made, strained, cooled and kept in covered containers in the fridge for up to three days in advance. Add the quartered lemon and orange slices just before serving.

AGA Bring to the boil on the boiling plate, cover and transfer to the simmering oven for about an hour.

Iced Tea

Very refreshing, especially on a hot summer's day.

SERVES 4-6
(MAKES 750ML/1 ¼ PINTS)
Preparation time 5 minutes

3 ordinary tea bags
150ml (¼ pint) boiling water
600ml (1 pint) bottled still water,
  cold
3 tablespoons caster sugar
ice cubes
slices of lemon, if liked

1 Put the tea bags into a large heatproof jug or bowl. Pour over the boiling water and leave for about 5 minutes.

2 Remove the tea bags, pour in the cold water and add the sugar. Stir.

3 To serve, put an ice cube in a glass and pour the tea over. Garnish with lemon if liked.

GOOD THINGS TO KNOW *It is important to use bottled cold water as sometimes water from the tap can leave a scum which floats to the top.*

AND ANOTHER THING *For variations, use Earl Grey, or some of the types of Indian or China teas.*

Bellini

A peach version of Buck's Fizz, which is delicious! We did test it whizzing up some peaches in a processor but it was too bitty. It's much smoother with bought peach juice.

SERVES 4
Preparation time under 5 minutes

100ml (4fl oz) peach juice from a
  bottle
300ml (½ pint) champagne

1 Mix the two ingredients together – it's as easy and delicious as that!

GOOD THINGS TO KNOW *This can be made with sparkling white wine too, but we prefer it with champagne.*

Lemon and Lime Fizz

This drink is very similar to lemonade, but with a lime twist.

SERVES 4
(MAKES 750ML/1 ¼ PINTS)
Preparation time 10 minutes

1 lemon, quartered
1 large lime
3 tablespoons caster sugar
4 ice cubes
750ml (1 ¼ pints) fizzy water

1 Whiz the lemon and lime together in a processor until roughly chopped. Add the sugar and ice cubes and whiz again until finely chopped.

2 Carefully add the fizzy water and whiz.

3 Strain the liquid through a sieve into a large jug.

4 Pour into four glasses and serve.

GOOD THINGS TO KNOW *Do make sure you pulp the lemon and lime first and then add the fizzy water. If you try and add it all together, it will pour out of the top of the processor.*

Gunners

This is one of my husband's favourite drinks. After every round of golf, he has this at the 19th tee!

SERVES 2
Preparation time 5 minutes

600ml (1 pint) ginger beer
100ml (4fl oz) lime cordial
a few drops of Angostura bitters
ice cubes, to serve

1 Pour the ginger beer and lime cordial into a small jug.

2 Add a few drops of Angostura and stir well.

3 Put a few ice cubes into two large glasses and pour over the drink.

GOOD THINGS TO KNOW *This really needs to be made and served straightaway, otherwise the fizz will be lost from the ginger beer.*

MB Bomber

We devised this drink after a long day's work, and it is very refreshing. Just try it – it's delicious!

SERVES 4
(MAKES ABOUT 450ML/16FL OZ)
Preparation time 5 minutes

300ml (½ pint) cranberry juice
150ml (¼ pint) bitter lemon
2 tablespoons dark rum
ice cubes, to serve

1 Mix all the ingredients together in a large jug.

2 Pour into glasses with a cube of ice.

GOOD THINGS TO KNOW *It can be made with low-calorie, diet bitter lemon.*

Index